Phoenix

The Fateful Journey

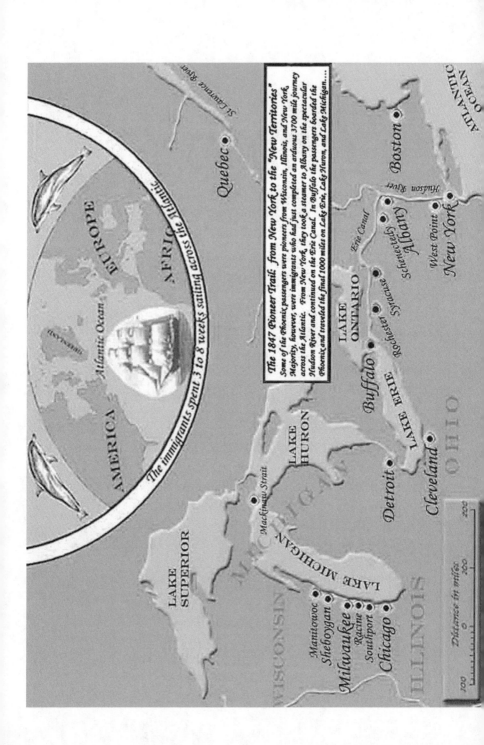

The 1847 Pioneer Trail from New York to the "New Territories"

Some of the Phoenix passengers were pioneers from Wisconsin, Illinois, and New York. Majority, however, were immigrants who had just completed an arduous 3700 mile journey across the Atlantic. From New York, they took a steamer to Albany on the spectacular Hudson River and continued on the Erie Canal. In Buffalo the passengers boarded the Phoenix and traveled the final 1000 miles on Lake Erie, Lake Huron, and Lake Michigan....

The immigrants spent 3 to 8 weeks sailing across the Atlantic

Phoenix

The Fateful Journey

The True Story of Immigrant
and American Passengers Traveling in 1847
Aboard a Doomed Steamship

John Textor

SANDERLING PRESS

www.phoenix1847.com

PRINTED IN THE UNITED STATES OF AMERICA

First edition published 2006

ISBN 0-9773710-0-X
LCCN 2005908849

ATTENTION CORPORATIONS, UNIVERSITIES, SCHOOLS, AND PROFESSIONAL ORGANIZATIONS: Quantity discounts are available on bulk purchases of this book for educational, gift purchases, or as premiums for increasing magazine subscriptions or renewals.

For information, please contact
Sanderling Press
PO Box 436, Sheboygan
WI 53082-0436
or e-mail: Info@Phoenix1847.com

To the memory of those who perished and in tribute to those who survived. Like the ancient phoenix, a few emerged out of the flames and ashes to fulfill the dreams of seeing their descendants live in freedom and prosperity.

PREFACE

Two hours before dawn on November 21st, 1847, the steamship *Phoenix* was just eight miles away from Sheboygan, its next destination in Wisconsin. Starting in Buffalo, the ship had spent nine days in stormy weather crossing Lake Erie, Lake Huron, and finally Lake Michigan. Aboard were about three hundred passengers and crewmen.

The *Phoenix* was one of the most modern ships of its day, utilizing the recently invented propellers instead of side-wheels. The ship's name was based on the mythical bird from the ancient Middle East, said to live for 500 years. As it's end approached, legend held that the phoenix was consumed by fire in its nest. From the flames and ashes, a new phoenix would miraculously emerge.

Like its namesake, the *Phoenix* and its passengers would also be tested by fire. This is the true story of the passengers and their fateful journey. All events and names are all factual. Much of the dialogue and journey descriptions were recreated based on the letters of other immigrants and pioneers traveling during the same period.

CONTENTS

Chapter 1

The Quest for Freedom and Prosperity

Rotterdam, Illustrated London News, 1847

In 1847, life was hard in Holland. Once again, potatoes were afflicted by blight and other food was scarce and expensive. Large families lived on small farms and there were few other job opportunities. People often talked about America where land was cheap and life full of luxuries. Few were prepared, however, to begin a new life across the Atlantic. One reason was that the emigrants were not likely to ever see their relatives and friends again in Holland. Another deterrent was the long dreadful journey with storms and sea monsters menacing the frail ships.

Gerrit Geerlings was one of the most respected residents of Enter, a small Dutch town located a hundred miles east of Rotterdam. He operated a well-known flour mill and had served earlier as a deacon in his church. Forty-four years old, of average height and slightly paunchy, he was strong and could pick up a sack of grain with one hand. A copious beard and dark parted hair framed an oblong compassionate face. Geerlings' home, already lively with six of his children, was a popular meeting place for neighbors seeking spiritual guidance. Their conversations often focused on the emigrants who had established new life in America.

Geerlings spent many late evenings reading booklets on the Dutch pioneers describing their journeys and the settlements in America. The majority of emigrants were farmers who dreaded the three to eight weeks spent on a sailing ship crossing the Atlantic. At night and during stormy weather, "steerage" passengers were confined to the dark cargo compartments filled with foul air. After a couple of weeks, food would be limited to moldy bread, watery stew, and putrid water. On most transatlantic passages, several ship passengers would die.

Upon arrival in New York, most pioneers boarded ships that would take them west to the New Territories. The trip up the Hudson River took a full day and was followed by ten days on the Erie Canal. The final week of the journey was spent on a steamship, traveling over a thousand miles on the Great Lakes to Wisconsin or Michigan. In their letters home, the pioneers urged others to join them but also cautioned about traveling late in the season when storms were common.

Dutch newspapers described Wisconsin as wild frontier territory where hostile Indians outnumbered the settlers and where freezing winters and hardships prevailed. Hard work was necessary to clear the virgin land, which in most cases was covered with thick forests. Nonetheless, the pioneers described it as a land of great opportunities. Once cleared of trees, the soil was fertile and wheat and corn grew readily. Land purchased from the government for $1.25 per acre would be worth several times more once it was made cultivable. Prices near the larger communities were generally between ten and thirty dollars per acre.

Life in the New Territories was flourishing. Between 1837 and 1847, Milwaukee's population exploded from one thousand to fourteen thousand. Chicago was even larger, with a population of almost twenty thousand. Numerous ships crisscrossed the Great Lakes, bringing reasonably priced hardware and taking produce to the consumers on the East Coast.

To Geerlings, the greatest attraction was the fact that the settlers were guaranteed freedom of religion. Most of the recent Dutch pioneers in America were the "Seceders" from the Reformed (State) Church. In the past few years, small groups had left the old world to avoid religious persecution and to escape deteriorating economic conditions. In many ways, the Seceders resembled the English Puritans who were among the earliest settlers in America.

A year earlier, Gerrit Geerlings considered emigrating to America with the first large Seceder group led by the Reverend Albertus Van Raalte. The idealistic life in a Seceder community was very appealing to Gerrit but his wife Aaltje, later known as Eliza, refused to leave their homeland. She was accustomed to urban life and did not care to join the pioneers living in primitive log cabins. Her father, Willem de Vries, was a prosperous miller who shared some of the Seceder sentiments but was opposed to emigration. Eliza remembered his reprimands as to what would happen to Holland if everybody with a grievance or wanderlust were to leave the country.

In earlier years, Geerlings was an inspiring deacon in Hattem where he worked closely with the Seceder leader

Reverend Anthony Brummelkamp. Initially, the fiery Brummelkamp merely criticized the new regulations imposed by authorities on the state church. The autocratic Dutch king had already alienated people by increasing taxes to pay for fighting rebels in the Dutch colonies and the breakaway Belgium. The dissident Reverend was removed from his church position but his followers continued to meet on private sites. The authorities retaliated by levying heavy fines when more than twenty worshippers gathered. At times they even quartered troops in the homes of leading preachers to restrain contacts with their followers

Eventually the Geerlings moved to Enter where, with his father-in-law's money, he became established as a miller. Gerrit Geerlings led a comfortable life but remained inspired by the Seceder beliefs. He sought out other sympathizers in the area to share together their spiritual quest in his home.

Geerlings' yearning for America was rekindled in the spring of 1847. His oldest son Albert had decided to emigrate to avoid the oncoming military service. It was a very painful decision for a young man. Family members who emigrated to America were unlikely to ever see their relatives or friends again. Geerlings certainly did not want his son to move so far away. The alternative was even worse, however, as the government was likely to send him to fight in the Dutch East Indies colonies.

Soon after Albert left, Eliza showed the first sign that she was considering following her son to America. She told her husband that she had read the pamphlet, "Voices from North America with a Foreword by A. Brummelkamp," left behind by their son, Albert. It was a collection of letters from the pioneers describing their journeys and life in Michigan and Wisconsin. Eliza had mixed feelings about the New Territories around Lake Michigan, which were favored by the Dutch emigrants. She liked the spirit of freedom but loathed the hardships of the settlers' life.

For weeks Geerlings did not hear his wife mention America again. At the time, however, all their attention was centered on their latest offspring. Their daughter Alberta was born on June 2nd and, from birth, she was weak and had trouble breathing. A premonition descended on both parents. They had a total of fourteen children but six of them had died before reaching one year of age. Thirteen days later, Alberta also passed away. Eliza went into shock, refusing to answer questions or greetings. Right after the funeral, she surprised her husband by telling him to make arrangements to travel to America. She wanted a new start for their family in Milwaukee where her husband could work as a miller.

Dutch emigration to America in 1847 was running at a rate five times higher than during the preceding years. Groups were banding together, determined to leave misery and oppression behind them. Newspapers reported that ships were fully booked but that arrangements were being made for additional vessels. Geerlings disliked traveling late in the season because of stormy seas and cold weather on arrival. However, waiting until the following year involved the risk that another childbirth would delay them again.

In any case, it was desirable to travel in a group with other Seceders. Most potential emigrants were farmers waiting to harvest their fields to earn money for travel and expenses in America. Using his contacts, Geerlings arranged for a ticket agent to visit their town and describe the available post-harvest voyages.

Economic conditions were precarious that summer in Holland and elsewhere on the continent. In the previous two years, potato crops had been devastated by blight, sending food prices soaring. The outlook for the oncoming harvest remained questionable. Most farmers had large families and small farms. A person with three cows was considered rich. At the same time, there were very few non-farm jobs for the young people. Employment of the textile weavers was being reduced, impacted by the new English mills, and weavers' wages kept dropping lower. Young girls had to work as maids just to receive food and a bonus ten dollars a year, paid to her parents.

While most people lived in misery, Hendrikus Swijtinck was actually prospering as a ticket agent. For each transatlantic passage, he received a four-dollar commission. During the previous year, he had sold less than forty tickets but still earned twice as much as an average farmer. In 1847, Swijtinck expected to sell two hundred tickets. However, the prices for large groups were discounted and his commission was between one and two dollars. The ticket agent did most of his business with the Seceders, who no longer needed much persuasion to go to America. They had even formed their own society to loan the travel money to those who could not afford to go.

Swijtinck was so busy that normally he would not consider traveling to Enter to drum up more customers. The Seceder leaders told him, however, that Geerlings had a large family and that there were other neighbors interested in emigrating. He decided it would be worthwhile to make an effort to pass through their town.

Two weeks later, the ship-booking meeting was held at Geerlings' home shortly after the evening meal. Ten of Geerlings' Seceder sympathizers were invited, along with their wives. In the whole group, there was not one person who had ever seen the sea. Most of them had lived their whole lives in the same community and had never traveled overnight away from their homes. The men, the majority of them farmers, had wary looks on their faces and came prepared with a lot of questions.

Swijtinck had witnessed and overcome such anxieties many times. Middle-aged, tall and calm, there was an air of authority exuding from him. He reminded his listeners that, in making their decision, they needed to consider their children's prospects. If they stayed in Holland, their daughters would work as maids or marry other poor farmers. Their sons would be sent to chase rebels in the Dutch colonies or fight in other wars, which were certain to come. Their alternative was to go to America where everybody was equal and hard work would be rewarded with a prosperous life and religious freedom.

The talk soon centered on the cost of the journey and the anticipated expenses in America. The conversion rate was four dollars for the ten-guilder gold coin, which for many men, was a monthly salary. The cost of the transatlantic passage was about fourteen dollars per adult, with one ticket required for two children between the ages of three and fourteen. This fare was for the "steerage" passengers who slept in the cargo compartments and had to bring aboard their own food. In total, the cost for the travel to Rotterdam, food required for the ship, and the transatlantic ticket would amount to about twenty-six dollars per adult.

Swijtinck knew that Geerlings was a miller and that his family could probably afford to cross the Atlantic as cabin passengers. The tickets would cost about twice as much, however, and cabin passengers were restricted from mixing with the steerage passengers. In Swijtinck's experience, all Dutch emigrants, even the wealthy ones, traveled as steerage passengers and saved money to buy more land in America

The ticket agent continued his presentation by explaining the emigrants' anticipated expenses on the other side of the Atlantic. From New York to Milwaukee, each passenger would spend an additional dollar to travel up the Hudson River, five dollars on the Erie Canal, and another five dollars for the ship passage on the Great Lakes. More money would be needed for food and lodging between the connecting trips. All together, a family with four children needed about one hundred sixty dollars for all travel and food from Holland to Wisconsin. An additional several hundred dollars would be needed to purchase the land, build a cabin, buy the planting seeds and supplies, and to cover living expenses until the first harvest.

As Swijtinck paused, a man stood up. Hendrikus Lubbers, appeared shocked by the prices and was ready to leave. Lately, his earnings as a shoemaker were less than fifty dollars per year and he had hardly any savings. He looked at Swijtinck and sadly shook his head.

"I could never afford the money for the passage, not to mention the additional money to buy land. I might as well leave now."

Swijtinck walked up to the man and placed his hand on his shoulder.

"My good fellow, you can't afford not to go. Many of your friends here will sell their farms and have more than enough for their journey. It will be safer for them to loan you the money rather than carry all the gold coins with them. Borrow the money and take your family to Milwaukee. There are a lot of Germans there and you should be able to communicate with them. You can get a job earning a dollar a day. Pay off your debt and provide a bright future for your family. You will never be poor again and the authorities will never tell you what church you have to go to."

Thinking over the agent's words, the shoemaker Lubbers slowly sat down, as heads around him nodded. After a pause, the farmers in the group started to ask questions about the land in the New Territories. Was it really possible to buy the land from the government for $1.25 per acre? Would it be useful land or just marshes and forest wilderness?

Swijtinck stated that both open prairie land and wooded land were available in the Wisconsin and Michigan areas favored by the Seceders. Most pioneers preferred the forested tracts because the land was very fertile and the wood was useful for building homes. A lot of government land was still available at the official prices but it would not last long. In Michigan, speculators had already bought out most of the land. The Van Raalte's group recently settled on the eastern shore of Lake Michigan and had to buy most of their land from speculators. Fortunately, Van Raalte was able to negotiate a joint purchase at just over two dollars per acre.

In Wisconsin, Swijtinck explained, land was still readily available at the government price, at least in the more remote parts of the state. Whole sections remained unpopulated after the government had forced an 1837 treaty on the Indian tribes and ordered them to the northern part of the state. The agent urged the group to emigrate this year. A lot of Yankee and German farmers were starting farms in Wisconsin and soon all the good land would be sold.

A farmer shook his head, unconvinced about the prospects in far away America.

"I've read a newspaper article stating that the virgin prairie land is so tough and full of roots that it takes eight to ten oxen to pull a plow. In wooded sections, it takes months to clear a single acre of land. After buying land, most settlers simply don't have enough money to buy a pair of oxen, the proper farm implements, and other supplies needed to develop a successful farm. Even in the cleared sections, deep tree roots remain in the ground making it difficult to till. The plow often breaks or needs repairs. Meanwhile the pioneers live for years in tiny shacks, subsisting like wild beasts"

The group grew quiet and turned anxiously toward the agent to await his response. Swijtinck took time to consider the question. It was a tough group and there was no point in belittling the allegations. He finally calmly replied.

"The newspapers are under pressure by the government to print the most negative descriptions of America. It is true that a farmer who has little money for seeds will not gather a large harvest. Dutch pioneers in America like to buy as much land as they can, perhaps eighty or even one hundred sixty acres. Most of them spend the first autumn and winter clearing two to four acres of land. Remember that even wooded tracts have some meadows or areas covered with light brush. The first harvest will be enough to feed the family, with some left over for sale to the market. As more land is cleared, the life will change from subsistence farming to prosperity. Dutch settlers are hard workers and I don't know of any who have failed in America."

Swijtinck surveyed the room. He found a mixture of skepticism and curiosity on the faces of the Seceders. The rest of the evening was filled with more questions about the journey and life in America. The agent could sense that only a few of them were really ready to emigrate that year. Perhaps life in their small town was just too placid, with little religious bigotry and government interference. It did not help that Gerrit Geerlings, their spiritual leader, did not plan to share a pioneer life with other Dutch settlers. His wife Eliza had a penchant for city life and wanted to live in Milwaukee.

It was already dark when Swijtinck finally decided to draw the meeting to a conclusion.

"Everybody here dreams of a prosperous life in America. At the same time, you are reluctant to leave relatives and friends behind. Some of you will just keep on dreaming, hoping to emigrate, perhaps in a year or two. The trouble is that, in a few years, the cheap fertile land in America will no longer be available. Others among you will turn your dreams into a reality right now. You will travel to America together with other groups of Seceders from all over Holland. In a few years, you will be able to send the passage money to your relatives and friends so they can also share in the prosperity. For those of you who are ready, now is the time to step forward and secure your families' future."

Geerlings nodded his head and waited as other husbands and wives turned to each other. The whole room was filled with hushed discussions. After a few minutes, one of the farmers approached Geerlings and expressed his readiness to book the passage. Geerlings was happy that they would travel in company and turned to the agent to make his announcement.

"I am ordering tickets for myself, my wife, and our six children. We want to see our son in America and never worry about our other children being sent to a war."

Gerrit Hommers, a quiet widower who had listened intently to all the discussions, made the second ticket purchase announcement. "I have a fairly prosperous farm here but I want a new start for myself and my three children. I will be ready to travel after the harvest is completed and the crops are sold."

The shoemaker Hendrikus Lubbers looked at his wife Maria and she quietly nodded her head. Lubbers walked up to Swijtinck and said that his family would go if they could get a loan for the passage money for himself, his wife, and four children. The rest of the group continued talking with each other but remained unprepared to make such a momentous decision.

The next day, before Swijtinck left town, Geerlings and Hommers visited the town financiers and arranged the ship passage money for all three families. Hommers' farm and Geerlings' properties were to be sold by the end of the first week of August.

Chapter 2

Wisconsin

"The Early Settler Life" by Crabtree Publishing Company

On both sides of the Atlantic, travelers were planning journeys, which would culminate in the final voyage aboard the fateful *Phoenix*. The two young Hazelton sisters were from Sheboygan, Wisconsin. One of the fast growing ports on Lake Michigan, Sheboygan was a natural stopover for ships heading for Milwaukee fifty-five miles further south. The sisters moved to Sheboygan only a year earlier when their father had become the proprietor of the Merchants Hotel.

Hiram Hazelton was a jovial man with a drooping moustache who mixed easily with the stream of merchants, mariners, and travelers passing through his hotel. He moved to Sheboygan because it was a young fast-growing community. The first permanent white settlement was a sawmill, built in 1834. Three years later Sheboygan was the center of a speculative bubble with city lots selling for several hundred dollars. Some choice lots were actually sold to Yankee investors for as much as ten thousand dollars. Several dozen buildings were built and then by 1840 were mostly abandoned as the speculative boom was temporarily reversed.

New waves of pioneers and speculators followed and in 1847 the population reached one thousand people. Many Indian villages still remained in the area because the government did not enforce their eviction until the land was surveyed and sold. Groups of Indians wandered through the streets and often spooked Sheboygan residents by staring through their windows. The community was still surrounded by forests, which provided wood for buildings and fuel for the visiting steamships.

Mrs. Hazelton was devoted to her family but had a more conservative outlook on life than her venturesome husband. She agreed to move to the New Territories even though she missed the amenities of big city life on the East Coast. Currently her main concern was the education and social prospects for their two daughters. Eliza was fourteen and needed to learn more about literary classics and social graces. Even eleven-year-old Anne had outgrown the local school. Most of the students there were rowdy, younger children and they were all crowded into a single classroom. The teacher did her best to teach all students but concentrated mainly on spelling and arithmetic.

Things would change soon, however. Earlier in the afternoon, Mrs. Hazelton picked up a letter from her sister in Buffalo. A big smile appeared on her face as she read the long-awaited news. Arrangements were finalized for Eliza to stay in the boarding school for young ladies from proper families. Her sister also passed on the school principal's recommendation for the younger Anne to join Eliza at the boarding school. The two sisters were always very close and being together at school would somewhat ease the pain of separation from the parents.

The suggestion was sensible but Mrs. Hazelton knew that her husband was totally unprepared for it. He would do anything to fulfill the daughters' whims and they, in turn, adored his suppertime tales about sea captains and mountain men. It took a long time to persuade him to initiate the arrangements for Eliza to go to boarding school. How could he adjust himself to life with both daughters away from home?

"Hiram, the school principal recommends that both girls go to the boarding school together."

Hiram Hazelton turned his head toward his wife but remained silent for a long time. A grimace appeared on his face. The prospect of the girls' departure was not totally unforeseen, even if it was earlier than expected. Like many fathers, Hiram spent many nights wondering what kind of husbands their daughters would marry and how far away they would live.

Still dazed, Hiram finally protested feebly, "I am not even sure that Eliza is old enough to be away at boarding school. Anne is definitely too young."

His wife shook her head vehemently, determined to see to it that their daughters were exposed to finer education and social life. "Hiram, we both have seen Eliza jesting with young men. Her prospects in Sheboygan are to marry a sailor or a farmer. Eliza definitely needs to go away to expand her education and meet more socially acceptable young men. Anne is still very young but would also benefit from a better education. By being in school together, our daughters can support each other. Afterwards, they will return and we will be all reunited."

The mostly one-sided discussion continued for some time.

In the end, Hiram simply agreed to observe how Anne would react to the proposal of joining her sister at the boarding school.

Early in the evening the whole family gathered in the dining room for their supper. The girls quickly sensed that there was something serious to be revealed soon. Their father sat sullenly throughout the meal with none of his usual tales. After the solemn meal, Mrs. Hazelton spoke, describing the schoolmaster's recommendation that both sisters attend the boarding school together.

The usually sprightly Anne could hardly contain her resentment. "I am too young to be away from home and I don't see why Eliza needs to go to the boarding school. She reads a lot of books, is very pretty, and is going to marry a ship's captain. I will likewise read plenty of books so I can marry a captain of a big steamship. Please don't send either one of us away."

Their father remained silent while Mrs. Hazelton replied. "Steamship captains meet young girls in every port but will marry only young ladies with a proper education. Eliza, we have already decided on your boarding school plans and there will be no more debate about it. Still to be decided is whether you, Anne, will join your sister at the school now or in a year or two."

Anne raised more spirited arguments, followed by pleading and periods of stubborn silence. It took her some time to finally realize that her mother really meant what she had said. Anne's face was tense and resolute when she announced her final choice.

"If Eliza really has to go to the boarding school, I will go with her. Father, you will have our mother to comfort you; Eliza should not be alone at school. All I ask is that we can come back to spend Christmas at home."

Hiram Hazelton was touched by his young daughter's resolve and concern for those she loved. He reminded her, however, of the full implications of her decision.

"Anne, I will not stand in your way, if you really feel you need to go with your sister. But if you do so, you must be prepared to stay until the following year. You know that there are no ships during the winter to bring you home for Christmas. November is the end of the sailing season on the Great Lakes and even those journeys are hazardous because of late-season storms. Do you really want to go with Eliza?"

Anne took turns studying the faces of her father, mother, and Eliza. She finally replied, "If we have to go to boarding school, we will go together."

• • •

David Blish, another future *Phoenix* passenger, lived ninety-six miles south of Sheboygan in Southport, later renamed Kenosha. Southport was an even younger community than Sheboygan. In 1835, a group of adventurous investors from New York decided to start a colony in the magnificent New Territories. An advance party traveled to Milwaukee and was told of the unoccupied river-mouth sites near the Illinois border.

The pioneers eventually settled at the site where the Pike Creek emptied into Lake Michigan. In order to expedite housing construction, the settlers bought fifty thousand feet of lumber in Sheboygan. The lumber was brought by ship, thrown into the lake, and floated ashore in rafts. By the end of the first summer, more than a dozen dwellings were built.

That September, five hundred Indians temporarily joined the local population. The voyagers were on their way home from Chicago where they had received payments from the Federal Government. Forced by bad weather to land their canoes, the Indians spent three weeks trying to live off the land. Eventually the settlers roasted an ox for the starving

Indians and were happy to see them depart.

Southport grew quickly, being a natural stopover for ships crossing Lake Michigan on the way to Chicago. In 1847, the population numbered three thousand people. Thirty-three year old David Blish, born in New Hampshire, moved first to Green Bay and then, in 1843, to Southport. He had made money on wise real estate investments and owned docks and warehouses. His passion, however, was his lumber business which was very successful almost from the start. The prices were fair and Blish quickly became known for his friendly manners and knowledgeable advice about construction and repairs.

Sundays were the only days when the Blish family enjoyed leisurely dinners together. David's young attractive wife was also a good cook and invariably prepared a delicious meal. After dessert David remained at the table sipping tea while his four children crowded around him. His six and four-year-old sons wanted to hear tales about the colorful pioneers visiting his lumber store. The two-year-old daughter and the small infant son were content just to rock on his knees.

On the last Sunday in September 1847, David Blish was in a particularly festive mood. During the week he had received large orders for lumber from two farmers. One of them also told an interesting story.

"Mr. Fink tells me that he owns a set of chains and is always being asked to loan or sell them. Most farms are still heavily forested and chains are a necessity for dragging the cut-down trees with oxen or horses. After harvest, Fink and his wife are planning to visit their relatives on the East Coast. It will be their first trip back home since moving to the New Territories. It will be also their chance to shop for things not available in Southport."

Blish turned to his wife and continued. "I have been considering previously adding more hardware to our lumber business. Mr. Fink made me realize how important the tree-dragging chains are for the development of our county. I decided to take a trip next month to the East Coast to buy chains, nails and other hardware directly from the manufacturers."

He saw a frown on his wife's face and quickly added that it would also be an opportunity to buy some furnishings and luxuries for their home.

Mrs. Blish questioned the need for the trip. "You know that I have always supported your ventures but why go on a purchasing trip, which is bound to last more than a month? The warehouse hardware can be ordered by mail."

It was difficult for her husband to restrain his enthusiasm, "Honey, I want to get the chains and supplies before the winter since farmers do most of the tree clearing during the cold weather. It is too late to make arrangements for buying hardware by mail and still receive the shipment this year. Besides, I want to establish relationships with the best suppliers, thus reducing the cost of future purchases. There will be only one trip and the subsequent reorders would be handled by mail. Furthermore, the children need new clothes. We could also use a few luxuries for our home and real office furniture for our business. I will start the journey in the middle of October when business is slower and return before the end of November."

Concerned about the late sailing season known for nasty gales, Mrs. Blish asked, "Can't you wait until spring?"

Shaking his head, David reminded his wife that spring was the busy season and that he needed to have all the hardware before that. He then reassured her.

"The late-season storms on the Great Lakes have been a threat only to the sailing ships. A steamer takes a week to travel from Racine to Buffalo in New York. In bad weather it will merely take an extra day or so. Mr. and Mrs. Fink will be returning from their trip at the end of November. I will try to arrange so we can come back together."

•   •   •

Ten miles north of Southport was Racine, another booming Lake Michigan port with a population of three thousand residents. Captain Gilbert Knapp established the first settlement at the mouth of the Root River in 1834. A year later the New York pioneers deposited $2,700 to acquire all claims to the land in the area but legal quibbles prevented closing on the transaction. The New Yorkers then moved to the next river-mouth site, establishing Southport. Ever since those two communities were natural rivals.

Since its founding, Racine had attracted many adventuresome American pioneers plus immigrants from many European countries. Probably the most famous resident was Jerome I. Case who had revolutionized wheat harvesting, thus contributing to the growth of the New Territories. Case arrived from New York in 1842 with six of the "new-fangled" wheat threshers. There was a shortage of farm labor, so the machines designed to swiftly cut the grain were quickly sold. Jerome Case then proceeded to make a fortune by building even more advanced units. His new machines would further reduce labor by simultaneously cutting and separating the grain from the chaff.

Edwin West arrived with his wife in Racine in the early 1840s. During the first few years the wheat crops were plentiful, fertilized by the ash from the trees which were cut down and burned. In 1846, Mr. Case visited the West's farm and offered to sell him a thresher on credit. Mr. Case explained that the machine would pay for itself with the money earned during the harvest by working on the neighbors' fields. It was a tricky activity, however, as there were still many tree trunks remaining in the fields and they had to be located and bypassed.

Wheat farming in Wisconsin was a risky business as the rich virgin soil was easily depleted. In addition, there was always a risk of drought, which would occasionally devastate the fields. Many farmers diversified by planting the more drought-tolerant Indian corn but wheat remained the easiest crop to sell. West had gambled in 1847 by planting most of his fields with wheat and was richly rewarded with a bountiful harvest.

By the middle of September, most of the wheat had been sold, and Edwin West and his wife celebrated with a festive Sunday dinner. Edwin toasted their good fortunes with a glass of whiskey.

"Our life has been good in Wisconsin and our son has been born here. We have always planned to make a fortune and then move back to New York to live close to our families. Lately I've been thinking that I prefer to continue to live here and perhaps buy some additional land."

He noticed a frown on his wife's face and quickly resumed to mollify her objections. "We can still see our families every few years, in fact we can still visit them this year. I checked with our neighbors and they agreed to look after our farm while we are away. A steamship will be departing from Racine to Buffalo this Wednesday. We could take that ship, spend four weeks with our families in New York, and still get back before the winter."

Mrs. West was so excited about the prospect of seeing her family soon that she practically forgot her husband's revision of their long term plans. Her first response was simply, "Why just four weeks, why don't we spend the whole winter in New York?"

Her husband shook his head. "A long stay is out of the question. The steamships will not resume cruising on the Great Lakes in the spring until the ice melts on the rivers connecting the lakes. The late schedule would make me tardy in the preparations for the spring planting and could lead to a bad harvest."

In response, Mrs. West got up from her chair and embraced her husband. "Sweetheart, thank you for taking us to visit our families, regardless of how long we will stay there. It will be the first time my parents will see their two-year old grandson. It will also be nice to do some real shopping. I am just a bit concerned about returning late in November. We ran into some bad late-fall storms when we first came to Wisconsin."

Edwin gently kissed his wife before replying. "We came to Racine on a sailing ship. I remember very well that long and grueling passage. With current steamship service, things are different. Sailors say that storms are a threat to the sailing ships but not to the steamships. Furthermore, the ship leaving on Wednesday is a "propeller." It is the most advanced form of steamship, which uses screw propulsion rather than the more fragile side wheels. Darling, they assure me that the only danger of traveling in a storm is getting seasick."

• • •

The final Wisconsin passengers who would travel aboard the *Phoenix* were Mr. J. Long, his wife, and their young daughter. They lived in Milwaukee for several years and had made good money managing a general store.

Milwaukee became the largest town in Wisconsin because of the prime location. Three rivers emptied into the harbor on Lake Michigan and provided the vital in-land routes for the early voyagers. Solomon Juneau, a French-born fur trader arrived in Milwaukee in 1818 and married the granddaughter of the Menomonee Indian Chief.

The 1834 Indian treaty forced the natives to abandon their villages. Juneau bought out much of the eastern part of the current day Milwaukee. Byron Kilbourn from Ohio and George Walker from Virginia purchased large tracts of land of the west and south side of Milwaukee. Land speculation took over with town lots selling for hundreds of dollars. Fighting between rivals and financial panics caused some interruptions but did not stop the rapid growth. In 1846, the three founding fathers agreed to incorporate as a unified town with Juneau as the first mayor. The population stood at 9508 and, in the next ten years, would double.

Mrs. Long had an uncle in Chicago and, initially, wanted to move there. Her husband wanted to join his cousin in Milwaukee but agreed to investigate the prospects in both towns. Chicago was somewhat larger, with many opportunities and good connections to Mississippi and the rich prairie farmlands. Milwaukee also had good prospects and was considered a much healthier city. Chicago was built directly on the swamp ground, resulting in muddy streets and no sewers. Long read about the expensive fixes that had been proposed in Chicago. The level of the streets was to be raised and all the homes jacked up to add a higher foundation. Such an expensive project was likely to take a decade to finish and that's why they both agreed to settle in Milwaukee.

Their business was prospering and, at the end of summer of 1847, Mrs. Long pleaded with her husband to visit their families on the East Coast.

"I can't wait to see my parents and I want to show them their granddaughter. We were supposed to go last year but things were just too hectic. You promised me that we would travel this year and time is running out. We should leave in September when the weather is still warm and sunny so we enjoy the journey."

Her husband also wanted to visit their families but had been always reluctant to leave the business unsupervised. With time, he gained enough confidence in his chief clerk to consider him trustworthy and able to handle the business for a month or two. He agreed that they would travel soon.

"OK dear, we will depart before the end of September or as soon as I receive and pay for this large shipment I have been expecting."

His wife was happy that the decision to travel was finalized but a bit disappointed they could not leave in the next few days.

Mr. Long noticed the slight frown on her face and proceeded to cheer her up, "If there are no problems in the store during our absence, then we will travel to the East Coast again in a year or two...."

Chapter 3

Ireland

THE EMBARKATION, WATERLOO DOCKS LIVERPOOL

The Irish departing for America, Illustrated London News, 1850

Clarence O'Connor considered himself one of the luckiest men in Ireland. He had a pretty, hard-working young wife, a bright cheerful daughter, and a steady well-paying job. The whole neighborhood was proud of his achievement as the only Irish boiler engineer in a large knitting mill. True, his working hours were long: from six in the morning to seven at night, with Sunday the only day off. The important thing was that, in his house, there was always food on the table for his family and their relatives and friends.

Conditions were much worse in Ireland than elsewhere in

Europe. For most Irish farmers, potatoes were the primary source of nourishment. Two years of the devastating potato famine had caused widespread suffering. In one county after another a new type of blight would suddenly appear and quickly reduce entire fields of potatoes to rotted compost. With their crops ravaged, people turned to eating grass and bark.

The situation was made worse by the fact that large British estates owned much of the land. Many of the absentee landlords responded to the blight by converting the land to livestock grazing. Each month, thousands of the tenant farmers were simply evicted. Only the luckiest of those ex-tenants were given money or loans to emigrate to America. Some relief food shipments from America and England eventually arrived but hundreds of thousands of people simply had died of starvation.

Even those farmers still remaining on their land were looking forward with trepidation to the 1847 harvest. Prospects for that year were somewhat better but it would be a meager harvest at best. Many fields were not even fully planted, due to the high cost of the seed potatoes and the uncertain crop outlook.

The suffering in Ireland was reflected even in O'Connor's home. Every day hungry relatives and friends stopped by the house. Mrs. O'Connor usually kept on the stove a big pot of oatmeal or mashed Indian corn and each visitor would get a bowl. Often it was their only meal of the day.

Gone were the days of life without worries about expenses. Several years earlier, Mrs. O'Connor had inherited her father's farm and leased it out. The rent from the tenant was used for a few luxuries and the rest saved. For the past two years, however, their tenant farmer was hard pressed to make even token payments. Meanwhile, the O'Connors still had to pay the taxes on the land. Nonetheless, thanks to Clarence's job in the knitting mill, they were able to get by and had the satisfaction of helping those around them.

In the English-owned mills, not many Irishmen held such a responsible job as the boiler engineer. O'Connor started work at the knitting mill five years earlier as a material handler, delivering raw materials and moving the finished goods. The hub of the mill was the steam engine, which powered all the equipment. O'Connor had always been fascinated by the equipment and often paused by the boiler just to greet the engineer or ask him some question. The rhythmic clanking of the pistons was like music and helped to pace him through the long hours of work.

At Sunday family dinners, O'Connor was often asked to retell the story of how he prevented a boiler explosion, saving the lives of dozens of workers. He was not really sure when he first had become aware of the change in the sound made by the pistons and the released steam. It was a gradual change with a growing unfamiliar whistling tone. Twice he mentioned it to the boiler engineer. The usually tolerant Scottish engineer merely cussed him and busied himself feeding more fuel to the boiler. A nearby worker admonished O'Connor to leave the engineer alone as his son had died in an accident the day before.

As moments passed, the strange whistling tone grew slowly in intensity. O'Connor found the change unnerving and decided to bring it to the attention of the mill's chief mechanic. The man swore, ran to the boiler, and frantically started to pump water. Afterwards he commended O'Connor.

"The boiler was low on water and would have exploded any minute." Shaking his head, the man continued. "My cousin was killed in England when the boiler blew up and the whole mill was destroyed. O'Connor, you have a good ear and you sure demonstrated a lot of initiative."

The old boiler engineer was fired for his negligence and O'Connor was trained to take over the position. The promotion came soon after the start of the initial potato famine. The extra money helped to provide additional meals for his relatives and friends. O'Connor took great pride in his job and the respect he received from coworkers.

Reflecting on his job, O'Connor realized that the only negatives about his life were the awfully long working hours. The sole free day, Sunday, was never long enough. After church, there were always chores to be done around the house. After dinner, there were stories to be shared with the wife, relatives, and friends. O'Connor's stories rarely included exaggerations but many guests specialized in tall tales. O'Connor sometimes would whisper in his daughter's ear not to believe everything that was being told. Nonetheless, he enjoyed the exaggerations as an escape from the dreadful workweek spent at the mill.

Each year was divided into two seasons. From October until March, the mill workers would get up before dusk, work the whole day, and return home in darkness. During the other months, O'Connor could actually see some sunlight, at first only before work, and eventually before and after work. He had heard exciting rumors in the plant about new laws in England, which would limit work at the mills to ten hours a day. There was also talk that work on Saturdays would be limited to half a day. Skeptics among workers claimed that such laws would never extend to Ireland. Others warned that the English owners would rather close the mills than comply.

It was O'Connor's longing for more free time with his family that eventually got him into trouble. In August 1847, a new mill manager took over. On his first tour, he stopped by the boiler inspecting the equipment and asked questions about its operation. The manager said that he had heard about O'Connor's role in preventing the boiler explosion and complimented him on doing a good job.

Deceived by the manager's affable manners, O'Connor

abandoned his normally cautious instincts. "Aye, I love my job, even though I don't see my family much, except for Sundays. But I hear rumors that the mill hours may be shortened and that on Saturdays work may end at noon...."

The mill manager's face instantly changed to a scowl. "Give the Irish a chance to earn a good living and they will want more leisure immediately. More free time, just so they can get drunk Saturday evening. I hate people who start such rumors and I don't think much of those who spread them."

The manager studied O'Connor's face, pleased to see an expression of fright and confusion. Any sign of a rebellious stance would lead to an immediate firing. After a moment he continued, "Listen O'Connor, you can keep your job for the time being, if you give me the names of the troublemakers who have been spreading those rumors."

O'Connor swallowed hard before replying that he had heard it from people in town and that he did not know their names.

The answer seemed only to provoke further the mill manager's anger, "Sounds to me like you are covering up for those agitators.

The manager paused and then his face reddened. "I bet you are the one starting those rumors! You Irishmen think you're indispensable. Actually, it's just a matter of time before you will get drunk and cause an accident. You are fired! I want you out of this mill and I want you out of Ireland so you will not cause any more trouble here! Any wages that you have coming will be paid only if you show us a ticket to America."

The manager walked away leaving a stunned O'Connor standing next to his beloved boiler. A minute later the chief mechanic arrived and simply said, "O'Connor, I got you this job and you disappointed me. You don't have any future in this country; good luck in America."

Slowly, O'Connor started to walk away. The machinery

noise prevented the other workers from overhearing the conversations but they all knew his fate as he approached the exit
door.

On the way home, his main worry was how to break the
bad news to his wife. He was mad that the English did whatever they pleased in Ireland and did little to help the starving
people. At the same time, he was warming up to the idea that
he would have to go to America, the land of freedom and prosperity. The Irish in America would prove to the whole world
that they were enterprising and full of courage. Eventually, they
would return to Ireland and liberate it from the English.

O'Connor's early return immediately tipped off his wife
about the bad news. Her face grew pale and she listened silently
as he explained what happened at the mill. She shrieked
"never" when he tried to cheer her up describing their prospects
in America. She was determined that nobody would force them
out of their own country. She still owned her father's land and
they could survive living as farmers.

They had never discussed the possibility of emigrating to
America and thus he was surprised by her outright rejection. He
tried to reason with her and found that her main objection was
based on the terrifying stories printed in the newspapers. Ships
with Irish passengers were particularly prone to "ship fever",
later determined to be the typhus, spread by infected lice.
During the past year, tens of thousands of Irish emigrants had
died during the transatlantic passage, roughly one out of five of
those who traveled. Thousands more died soon after reaching
the American shores.

The newspaper articles carried stories of some ships where
most of the passengers and crew were stricken with the fever:
half of them would never recover. Upon arrival, port officials
inspected closely all Irish immigrants reaching America.
Anybody sick was either turned back or else placed in quar-

antine facilities where there was little chance of survival.

Mrs. O'Connor pleaded with her husband to remain in Ireland and take over her father's farm. "The crop prospects are much better this year. Surely, God will have mercy on us and not allow the blight to return. If you work on a farm, at least I will get to see you more often."

His wife's pleading caused O'Connor to reconsider the possibilities of making a living as a farmer. After all, he had spent the first twenty years of his life on his father's tenant farm. After he started working at the mill, he often dreamed about being outside in the fields while the sun was shining. Still, his instincts told him that the Irish potato blight was only in remission and was bound to come back.

"We can't risk our future by trying to live on your father's farm. The blight is bound to be back and the English will ruin us with their taxes. Because of the current improved crop outlook, the land prices have moved somewhat higher. Lets sell your father's farm while we have a chance to get a reasonable price. Then, we will go to America and decide whether I will work in a mill or whether we will buy a farm."

O'Connor continued, trying to persuade his sullen wife. "One of my coworkers at the mill has an uncle who has emigrated to Boston. The uncle's letters are full of advice for those contemplating the journey. The main point is to avoid ships carrying Irish emigrants to Canada or Boston. Fares to those destinations are the lowest, making them the primary destinations for the starving and sickly poor. Death rates on the ships going to New York are considerably lower. The lowest death rates are on ships carrying German and other continental passengers where the fatal ship fever is practically nonexistent."

He reemphasized the last point, "The ship fever is practically nonexistent among the continental passengers."

O'Connor's narrative seemed to mollify his wife's opposition to the transatlantic journey so he began to extol the prospects on the other side of the ocean. "My friend's uncle writes that the best opportunities in America are in the New Territories of Wisconsin and Illinois. Many Irish farmers have bought land in the hilly sections of Wisconsin. The land is covered by forests and is very fertile, once the trees are cleared. The farmers write that the land there reminds them of the hills in Ireland. Best of all, a lot of land tracts are still available at the cheap government prices."

O'Connor eventually convinced his wife that they would sail to New York from an English port. Once there, they would travel to the New Territories where cheap land could still be bought from the government. If they liked the conditions there, they would buy a farm and settle down. Otherwise, they could move on to Chicago and he would get a mill or factory job there.

Mrs. O'Connor agreed reluctantly, still afraid of the journey across the Atlantic. The dreaded fever often occurred even on ships leaving from the English ports. Nobody knew the cause of the disease but newspapers stated that the outbreaks were usually limited to the steerage passengers only. Mrs. O'Connor obtained an agreement from her husband that they would travel as cabin passengers. Although the tickets would cost twice as much as for the steerage passage, the family's safety came first.

When their departure day came a month later, O'Connor was excited but also regretful. It was difficult to leave relatives and friends behind. O'Connor hugged his cousins and promised to write and send them money as soon as he would get established in the New Territories. Everybody repeated that they would pray for a safe journey.

Among all the well-wishers, an old uncle grumbled that

soon all Irishmen would leave or die, allowing the English to completely take over Ireland.

A cocky young man disagreed. "Those of us remaining here will never allow that. It's just a matter of time before there is an uprising against the English. With justice and God on our side, and we will prevail."

The young man's declaration aroused strong emotions in O'Connor.

"I swear that I will return to fight the English once a rebellion becomes imminent. When the time is right, all Irish men from America will come back fully armed. I want to be a part of the uprising that will reestablish a free and prosperous Ireland."

Chapter 4

Holland

Rotterdam, Illustrated London News, 1847

As he was leaving Enter, the ticket agent Swijtinck was pleased with the results of his visit there. He had earned over twenty dollars in commissions by selling tickets for eight full fares and eight half fares. Most Dutch families would spend six months earning that amount.

From Enter, Swijtinck traveled to Rotterdam to check on the arrangements for additional ships. All Dutch ships sailing for America were already fully booked and even space on foreign ships was difficult to obtain. Fortunately, the firm he worked for, *Wambersie and Crooswijk,* had recently completed arrangements for an American frigate *France* to travel from Rotterdam to New York late in August.

Swijtinck's next stop was a small town of Winterswijk located on the German border in the province of Gelderland. The people there were among the most restless in Holland. Many townsfolk worked in Germany and brought back stories about successful German communities in America. The local Seceder activists eagerly awaited the ticket agent's visit and arranged a meeting on a farm of one of the followers.

The small barn was crowded and there were over thirty people gathered there. Swijtinck's entrance set off a round of polite applause. After greeting the men and women, he quickly proceeded to explain the costs for the journey and the expenses of setting up a farm in America.

The audience consisted mainly of modest farmers and it was obvious that they were anxious to start new lives in America. Most of the men had beards, wore somewhat tattered dark clothes, and already could pass for the pioneers from the New Territories. They greeted the shipbroker with a question, "What destination should we go to in America?"

Swijtinck was very familiar with the recent Dutch settlements in the Great Lakes area. The biggest was near Green Bay in upper Wisconsin. It was formed by Catholics, however, and therefore was of little interest to the Protestant groups.

The largest Dutch Seceder community, led by Reverent Van Raalte, was on the eastern side of Lake Michigan and would be later named Holland, MI. Most of the land there was forested, with some parts covered by marshes. Once cleared of timber, the land was very fertile. There was plenty of wood for building cabins, heating, and sale to the sawmills. Speculators, however, had already bought out all good land in that area. Any land close to that Dutch colony was likely to cost more than two dollars per acre.

Another large Seceder group had recently left for Pella, Iowa. The land there was mostly prairie and readily available but quite remote. After reaching Chicago, the settlers had to travel an additional three hundred miles by river and land. Swijtinck was not very enthusiastic about that destination. He stated that many farmers avoided prairies, seeking out forested tracts as a proof that the land was fertile.

In Swijtinck's opinion, the best prospects for the new Seceder groups were in Wisconsin. The government land was still readily available, at least in the more remote parts of the state. One group of Seceder settlers lived in Alto located ninety miles north of Milwaukee and about 40 miles west of Lake Michigan. The area was a mixture of fertile prairie land and wooded sections with plenty of streams.

Another group of Dutch families had settled in the southern part of Sheboygan County. The land there was mostly wooded and a few sections could still be obtained near the official government price. The prime tracts near Sheboygan, however, were already selling for more than ten dollars per acre. A lot of ships made stops there and the settlers could earn good money selling cords of wood to the steamships.

Swijtinck paused knowing how difficult it was for people in the barn to select the final destination based on his sketchy descriptions. Some emigrant groups would end up postponing that decision until reaching Sheboygan, their first potential location. If they liked that community and the land near it, they would stay. Otherwise they would proceed further.

Whatever would be their final destination, the farmers were eager to learn about life in the New Territories. "How do you buy land in America and what kind of harvests can be expected."

Swijtinck explained, "Eighty or one hundred sixty-acre tracts of virgin government land can be bought for $1.25 an acre, with the deed registered at the county office."

The farmers gasped in awe at the prospect of owning such

large tracts of land. They would have more than ten times the amount of land owned by their neighbors in Holland. It didn't matter that it would take decades of hard work to clear all the land.

The shipbroker's description of the harvests generated still further excitement.

"In America, all farmers have plenty to eat and earn enough money for other necessities and luxuries. The soil is fertile and a typical farm will produce as much as fifty bushels of wheat per acre. The price for wheat varies but I have heard that lately it's over $1.50 per bushel. The potatoes yields are also high but are hard to transport and are consumed mainly on the farm. Pork can be sold for twelve dollars per barrel. The timber from the land is also valuable for building homes and sale to the sawmills. Wood sold to the steamships fetches a dollar per cord, which is four feet wide, four feet high, and eight feet long."

Swijtinck also had to answer how the land would be cleared, especially if the farmers would not have enough money to buy draft animals.

"Work goes faster if the settlers have a pair of oxen, which cost about eighty dollars. In many cases several neighbors can pool their money together and then share their oxen. The virgin prairie land is tough but many settlers have tackled it without any oxen at all. Some pioneers buy their land and then work for others to save enough money to properly develop their own land."

The farmers and their wives also had a lot of questions on what they should carry with them on their journey. Swijtinck told them the size of the sea chests they could take with them. He also reminded them they had to bring along their own food for the ship journey. Drinking water was the only item that would be provided by the ship's quartermaster. Several cooking slots were available on each ship to allow the steerage passengers to make tea or cook simple meals.

The passengers also had to take along their dishes, cutlery, pots, bedding, and spare clothes. Most farm implements would be too bulky to carry and thus best left behind. They could expect the prices in the Midwest to be slightly higher but often the American farm tools were more suitable for the prairie soil. To save weight, they should discard the wooden handles for any axes, pitchforks, or hammers they wanted to take with them.

Another hour of questions and discussion passed. The only disappointment expressed by the farmers was that they would not travel on a Dutch ship. At the same time, they were curious about the American ship, which was to carry them. The newspapers reports from America always marveled about the number of steamships in service there. One of the men asked if they would be crossing the Atlantic on a steamship.

Swijtinck chuckled.

"Steamships require frequent refueling and thus are used only for rivers and shorter coastal trips. A few steamships did cross the Atlantic with the help of auxiliary sails. They had to carry so much fuel, however, that there was not much room left for cargo and passengers. In any case, currently the only available ship is the frigate *France*. It is a reputable American sailing vessel and almost all of the passengers will be the Seceders, just like your group. To insure the booking, I urge you to buy the tickets today."

There was only a short pause before the first man, Teunis Koffers responded. "I believe I am the oldest here. Being fifty-two years old, I don't need the government to tell me how and where to pray. I want to book the passage for me, my wife Berendina, and for our five children."

A murmur of approval spread among those in the barn.

Gerrit Guerkink was the next to make the announcement. "I am another 'old man' of forty-two years. My wife is no longer alive, but I will go with my five children so they can have a better life in America."

The Wilterdink family was next. Hendrik Wilterdink was going with his invalid wife, five children, and the family maid. Also going with them would be a recently married brother, Jan and his wife. A cousin, Derk Wilterdink, bought tickets for his wife, two children, and their farmhand. Another cousin, Herman Wilterdink, bought tickets for himself and his widowed mother.

Several other farmers proceeded to book their ship tickets. Jan Sikkink announced that he would be traveling with his wife, five children, and a maid. Also ordering tickets were the Onnink family of five, and the Esselinkpas family of eight. They were followed by the Kooyers family of four, the Te Winkel family of six, and the Nijweide family of seven.

There was another short pause before Jan Siebelink spoke up. "Holland is my homeland. I have a good farm and have only two children. We have taken in a neighbor's daughter as a maid and a youngster as a farm hand. We took them not because we needed help but primarily to help their families. I see that all my friends are leaving for America to provide a better future for their children. I am not going to remain the only one behind. I want tickets for myself, my wife Johanna, our two children, and our two helpers Janna Oonk and Gerrit Grevers. We will also help Janna's two uncles if they need help with their tickets."

Jan Oonk stood up and thanked Siebelink. He would buy his own tickets for himself, his wife, and their five children. The younger Gerrit Oonk could use some help, however, for tickets for his wife and their two children.

In addition to the thirteen families there were also three

unmarried people: Derk Voskuil, his cousin Berendina Willink, and Harmen Reuselink. All of them stated that they would go if they could get loans for the tickets. Derk Voskuil turned toward his sister Dora Nijweide and said that he hoped to get the loan from her husband. Berendina, a stepdaughter of Dora's uncle, also declared she would go if she could get a loan from Dora's husband.

There were still three farmers in the barn who did not state their intention to book the tickets. Slowly everybody turned toward them awaiting their decisions. The tallest among them was a stern farmer in his mid thirties who said that his father was too old and sick to travel. The other two men were also held back by the need to look after their elderly parents. Possibly in a few years they would be able to join the group in America. Or perhaps their children would go to America when they were grown up.

Soon after the meeting in Winterswijk, Swijtinck traveled to Holten in the province of Overijssel. The audience there was more skeptical and clearly concerned with the risk of crossing the Atlantic. One farmer expressed a list of concerns.

"I have read newspaper stories about the "ship fever", which sometimes would kill most of a ship's passengers and crew. I also read about sailing ships that would depart and never be seen again. Sailors swear that there are sea monsters, which can sink the ships and eat the travelers. How many passengers arrive safely in America?"

The ticket agent had come across similar concerns many times before. "The ship fever does exist but only on the ships carrying the sick destitute Irish passengers. Ships traveling from Holland arrive in America with very few if any passenger casualties. Sometimes one or two passengers may die from accidents or from illnesses, which would have claimed their lives even if they had remained home. As for the sea monsters, they exist only in the old exaggerated tales about disasters in faraway oceans. During the last century, very few ships have been lost crossing the Atlantic. Only a great storm or a careless fire can sink a modern sailing ship."

A few more questions were asked about the conditions in America. As the meeting was ending, Hendrik Landeweerd announced that he would buy tickets for his wife, three sons, and three daughters. Two other married Landeweerd daughters would also be traveling along with their husbands Teunis Schuppert and Berend Jan Wissink. The final local family going to America was Egbert Beumer, his wife, one child, and Egbert's stepbrother.

Beumer, the last person to buy a ticket, scoffed when asked by his friends whether he was afraid of dying during the ocean journey. "We live in Holland where storms have breached the dykes many times, with thousands of people dying in the floods. Why should we be afraid of the hazards of crossing the Atlantic? We must pray every day and the Lord will guide us through all the perils."

Chapter 5

Farewell to Europe

Dutch countryside, from an old Dutch ceramic

Saturday, August 21st, 1847 was the departure day for most of the Dutch emigrants who would eventually travel aboard the *Phoenix*. The early morning was filled with final packing turmoil and tearful farewells. There was a mixture of apprehension about the journey and optimism about the prospects in America. Siblings and cousins hugged each other, hoping that those remaining behind would travel to America in a year or two.

Many older parents were remaining behind, knowing they could never survive the rigors of the transatlantic journey. It was also unlikely that children would ever return or even come for a visit. One elderly father tried to say goodbye to his departing son but started to sob instead. The youngest son comforted the father and promised to take care of his farm for as long as the father was alive.

Last minute complications arose everywhere but were somehow resolved. The Te Winkel family in Winterswijk faced perhaps the most heart-breaking dilemma. Just before the departure date, Jozina Te Winkel got sick and had to stay in bed. Her husband Gerrit tried to obtain a refund of the ship's passage fare but was reminded that there were no refunds on the tickets.

Gerrit Te Winkel briefly considered proceeding to America with their four children and Jozina's sister who lived with them as a helper/maid. His wife would join them later, most likely the following spring. The expensive ship tickets were simply too valuable to be wasted. Jozina was frantic, however, and insisted on her husband remaining with her. To utilize the ship tickets, the four children were to travel to America accompanied by Jozina's two sisters, Berendina and Geertruid Ten Haken. Jozina and her husband would travel to join them the following year.

Slowly the groups of emigrants from the various communities started on their way to Rotterdam. The largest group from Winterswijk first traveled by horse carts to Arnhem. Their driver swore afterwards that he would never again carry the emigrants. It was simply too heartbreaking to hear the forlorn farewells and the answering cries from those left behind.

After reaching Arnhem, the group traveled by a river barge. For children and most of the adults, it was their first trip away from their district and they stayed on deck fascinated by the unfolding scenery. Late in the afternoon, it started to drizzle and soon the weather changed to a heavy rain. The barge eventually halted and most passengers lay awake, listening to the rain pounding the roof. As darkness fell, some children started to cry. A small girl whispered, "Mama, please let's go back home."

Calm was restored only after the elders started to recite the Lord's Prayer. Soon everybody joined in. Gradually, the spirit of perseverance replaced the lingering doubts of whether they were making the right decision. One by one, the emigrants fell asleep.

Early in the morning, a short Sunday prayer service was held. Teunis Koeffers asked the Lord to protect them during their journey. Other passengers prayed for the relatives left behind. The barge then resumed the journey while the passengers were forced by rain to stay in their compartments. A church-like atmosphere remained there for most of the day. The adults prayed, trying to suppress the lingering doubts about leaving their relatives and homeland forever.

As dusk approached, the rain temporarily stopped and the passengers eagerly streamed outside. The air was fresh and the scenery was a big diversion. The river generally was higher than the surrounding fields, held in its channel by raised riverbanks. Dozens of windmills spotted the countryside, pumping excess rain water from the low fields to the river above. Traveling by barge was still a novel experience for most of the emigrants. The sensation was almost like floating on top of the world.

Soon the darkness fell and the barge stopped for the second night. The children became more used to their nomadic routine and fell asleep quickly. Most of the adults did not get much sleep the previous night and they also were soon dozing.

Just before dawn the barge resumed its journey. It rained intermittently throughout the day and the emigrants spent most of the time in their compartment. Many adults were silent and looked dejected. The thirty-year-old Derk Voskuil decided to cheer up his relatives by describing the nice weather awaiting them in America. He told his sister Dora that according to his German friends with relatives in Wisconsin, summers in that region were usually sunny with little rain.

Dora's husband Hendrik Nijweide heard the comment but found only negative implications. "Sunny weather and shortage of rain will lead to meager crops. I don't recall any mention of dry weather in letters from the Dutch pioneers nor did the ticket agent ever talk about it. I probably would not have bought the ship tickets if I had been warned about the dry climate."

Voskuil tried his best to appease his brother-in-law. "I thought that with all our rains and gloomy weather, everybody would look forward to more sunshine. Don't worry about the crops. The German farmers in Wisconsin wrote about the sunny summers but usually reported good harvests. Their advice is to grow a variety of crops. During some really dry summers wheat does poorly but Indian corn and other crops are always abundant."

Next to Voskuil was Teunis Koffers, the fifty-two year old farmer who was the first to announce his decision to buy the ship tickets. Voskuil turned toward Koffers' fifteen-year-old Jan and cautioned that his name was going to cause him problems in America.

Jan wanted to know the reason.

Voskuil smiled. "In America, Jan is a girl's name. It will be wise for a young boy to change his name to John to avoid the confusion."

The older Koffers was insulted by the advice for his son to change his name. "We are traveling to America but will be living in a Dutch settlement. There is no need for Jan to change his name. Everybody in our Dutch colony will know that Jan is a fine lad."

Late in the day the rain stopped and the passengers gathered on top of the barge to savor fresh air. Many remained there even after darkness came and the barge halted for the third night of their journey. No stars were visible and there were only a few flickering lights visible from the nearby villages. The Dutch August nights lasted less than ten hours. The farmers worked hard during the day, went to bed soon after it got dark around nine PM, and got up at first light.

At the crack of dawn, the barge resumed the journey. Following old habits, many passengers got up even though there were no chores to perform. It would be their last day to watch the Dutch fields and countryside. The skies were cloudy and the wind was brisk. They passed one windmill after another all busily turning to pump the recent rainwater and keep the fields dry.

In the early afternoon, the barge finally reached Rotterdam. The travelers looked in amazement at the rows of three and four-story buildings lining the riverbank. The city had a large population of almost eighty thousand people. Still, it seemed that the barge had passed almost directly from the surrounding fields into the middle of the city.

Some city lads were loitering by the water and took delight in scaring the young bewildered emigrant children. One of the boys, who was perhaps fifteen year old, called out to the barge.

"You must be traveling to America, aren't you? Do you know that in the middle of the ocean there is a monster that can swallow a whole ship? The ship can be saved only if each family throws one child into the water. Which one of your siblings will volunteer to be sacrificed to the sea monster?"

The elders on the barge cursed the lads and threatened to go after them and whip them. The prankster knew that the men were unable to get off the barge and started to taunt the whole group.

"Ja, ja, the sea monsters will devour all Hollanders who have been eating fat herrings. But don't worry. If you have never eaten any fish, then your life will be spared."

A man leaned out of the window. "You youngsters should

be ashamed of yourself to give such a farewell to our departing countrymen. I know where you live and I will talk to your parents, so expect a good whipping. As for you children, just forget what those mean boys have been telling you. The largest sea creature is a whale. Even a whale could not sink the large ship that will be taking you across the Atlantic."

The boys scattered and the emigrants continued with no further disturbances, observing the imposing buildings facing the city canals. Finally, the barge reached a quay, lined with rows of trees. They stopped close to where their ship, the American frigate *France*, was already moored. The emigrants were happy to see that the ship was much larger than their barge, with tall masts towering into the sky. Such a magnificent ship could safely sail through the worst storms.

The families were fortunate that they could haul their baggage directly to the ship. The schedules of the sailing ships were not always reliable and some emigrants had to stay for days in the nearby boarding houses waiting for their ships to arrive.

The Winterswijk emigrants were anxious to see their ship accommodations but it took more than an hour before they were processed. The ship's clerk first checked their tickets and wrote their names and hometown information in a log. The steerage passengers were then issued mattress covers to be filled with straw, which could be purchased from the nearby vendors. The passengers also had to furnish the rest of the bedding. Finally, they had to confirm that they had funds to purchase the required list of food provisions. The shopping for food had to be completed the next day, as the ship would leave early the following morning.

At last the passengers were allowed to board the ship. They filed aboard carrying their heavy sea chests. Teunis Koeffers was the first to descend down the ladder to the new quarters.

The steerage compartment was a dark cargo hold with flimsy rows of three-level bunks. Groups from other communities were already occupying some of the spaces. All bunks by the ladder, where the lighting was the best, were already full. Koeffers updated the fellow travelers standing above him on the main deck.

"There is not much room here. Get some ropes so we can lower the sea chests and store them under the bunks. One member from each family will stay here to claim the bunks. The rest of the women and children have to stay on top until we finish storing the baggage."

Slowly the sea chests were stored in every available space, with some of them protruding into the narrow walkways. It was already dusk when the children and women were finally allowed to their new quarters. Helped by a few dim lamps, children picked their bunks, with the oldest clamoring to be on the top level. The tired babies quickly fell asleep. Other children sat on the their bunks watching with dazed eyes the turmoil as passengers were arranging their belongings and slowly settling down.

Their work done, most men went back topside to meet other passengers and share observations. The travelers from the different provinces stayed in their own groups but eagerly questioned the strangers around them. The majority of the people were Seceders who had bought tickets from the ticket agent Swijtinck. Several families bought the few remaining tickets earlier during the week. Among them were the two Loume brothers from Zeeland province, their wives and seven children. There were also two German families from Baden and Prussia.

A German-speaking Hollander asked the Prussians why they traveled so far overland instead of sailing from the German ports.

The tall Prussian hesitated before replying, "Our authorities don't look kindly on people wishing to move to America. The emigration permits are difficult to obtain and can be quite expensive. It was a lot easier for us to simply travel to the Rhine River and then to Rotterdam where nobody would check our papers."

A light drizzle started again and most of the lights were extinguished. The passengers started to return to the steerage compartment to settle down for the night. Some small children were still awake, hugging their mothers, or peppering them with questions.

"Why do we have to go to America? What will we do if the sea monsters will attack our ship?"

All across the compartment, the mothers tried to hush their children. "You heard the man saying that even a whale could not sink our ship. The reason we are going to America is so you will never go hungry. Now you should pray to our Lord so that all our relatives and friends will be able join us in America in the future."

Whispering and occasional cries continued through most of the night. After a few hours, the air in the packed compartment grew stale. It was a relief when the hatches were finally opened and the morning sunlight illuminated the steerage compartment.

The women were the first to go up the ladder and form lines to the four cooking slots on the main deck. Two of the slots were used only for boiling water. For many families, hot tea or coffee would be the only warm serving they would have on that day and on most other days during the transatlantic journey.

After breakfast, men and boys crowded near the mast where a poster was attached, listing the provisions necessary for the journey across the Atlantic. A Dutch-speaking ship's quarter-master summarized the requirements.

"Each adult person will have a minimum of 140 pounds of food, including 30 pounds of sliced and dried bread or biscuits, 50 pounds of potatoes, beans, and peas, 20 pounds of bacon and salted pork, 10 pounds of flour, 20 pounds of rice, 20 pounds of oatmeal, plus specified quantities of sugar, coffee or tea, butter, cheese, vinegar, and other items. Each family will also have their own metal dishes and cooking utensils."

Most farmers brought with them potatoes, flour, cheese and other homegrown food. The remaining products had to be bargained for with the Rotterdam merchants. As the men toured the nearby stores, they found prices to be expensive. Even the stores recommended by Swijtinck, their ticket agent, were priced higher than they had expected. In addition, they had to pay extra for the wooden food storage boxes specified by the quartermaster. The food required for the trip was to be kept aboard the ship under lock and the quartermaster would issue the daily rations to the passengers.

By late afternoon, all the purchases were completed. A quartermaster carefully inspected all the provisions and found a few families without the required amount of the salted pork and bacon.

The poor farmers explained, "We have brought with us extra quantities of potatoes and cheese. In our homes, meat is an expensive rarity served only on holidays."

The Dutch-speaking quartermaster was adamant. "All passengers must turn in the meat rations and other items on the list. The list of minimum provisions has been set by authorities to give the passengers the best chance to cross the Atlantic in good health. Cheese will get moldy after a couple of weeks and people will get sick eating only potatoes."

Neighbors offered some of their extra provisions and the

rest had to be bought at the nearby expensive stores. Eventually everybody turned in the required provisions.

Early in the evening, agent Swijtinck stopped by to check that everything was all right and wish the passengers good luck. He urged them to write back to their relatives about their journey and life in America. Their relatives would share their letters with others in the Seceder community. He also reminded them that New York was originally a Dutch colony and that there were still Dutch people there who would help them to start their new life in America.

Swijtinck's final goodbye was to the Geerlings family. The ticket agent stood up on a crate and motioned for Gerrit Geerlings to join him. The Seceder groups from the various towns gathered around Swijtinck as he introduced this prominent passenger.

"Gerrit Geerlings has served as a deacon and worked closely with Reverend Brummelkamp, the spiritual leader of all the Seceders. You men are lucky to have such an important spiritual leader traveling with you."

A large group immediately formed around Geerlings in order to pry him with questions about his destination and future plans. A great disappointment was voiced when Geerlings stated that he was planning to settle in Milwaukee. He had to explain that his wife was in poor health and could not survive the winter in a shack in the new Dutch settlements. Besides, he reminded them, Brummelkamp had called for Milwaukee to be the meeting place for the Seceders. Geerlings' house would be a stopping place for those without money to buy land and for future relatives coming to Wisconsin to join their kin.

It was their last night in Holland and, fortunately, the weather had cleared up. Families gathered on the deck watching the city lights and reminisced about their relatives and friends. Those who left their parents behind were particularly distressed. One man was tormented by the image of his father sobbing during the departure.

"I should have never bought the tickets to America. None of us will ever see our parents again. I would like my younger brother to join me in America but that will not happen for as long as our father is alive..."

Another man consoled him, "Your father will be happy when you will write him about your new farm and about grand-children doing well in the land of freedom and prosperity. You can send money so your father will never be hungry. When the time comes for your father to join our Lord, your brother will join you in America."

Young lads traveling with their parents had little remorse about leaving the grandparents or relatives behind. Some of them proudly explained to each other the grandiose plans to get rich in America and then visit their villages in Holland. One lad proposed a firm reunion date. Pointing to a nearby tavern with a "Red Lantern" sign, he stated, "Exactly in ten years, on August 25th, 1857, we will all meet in this tavern."

Near the ship's gangway was an old man with a cart full of fruit, carefully chosen to tempt the departing emigrants. Hearing the youngsters' declarations, he smiled.

"Young men, I have never heard of any Dutchmen return-ing for a visit from America. Perhaps in twenty years they will have big steamships capable of crossing the Atlantic. If the travel is quick and inexpensive, then perhaps some of you will return to visit your homeland. But in the meantime, my coun-trymen, this is your last chance to taste sweet Dutch pears and plums. Buy them now and save the seeds for planting in America."

Chapter 6

Crossing The Atlantic

Hellevoetsluis, the emigrants' last sight of Holland

Early in the morning on Wednesday, August 26th, the lines were cast off and the frigate *France* was towed out by a large rowboat. The sky was gray from heavy overcast but, fortunately, it did not rain. The ship cautiously followed the main channel on the Maas River. A crowd of emigrants gathered on the main deck and watched as the tall buildings of Rotterdam dwindled in size.

The Dutch-speaking quartermaster joined the passengers and pointed out Captain W. Myers and other ship officers anxiously watching the river traffic. The captain was a sturdy man in his fifties, with a grizzled beard and a pipe protruding from his mouth. The first mate was tall, perhaps thirty-five years old, and he briskly directed more than a dozen crewmen scurrying on the deck. The American sailors all seemed to be strong and healthy; most of them were taller than the Dutch travelers. The Dutch passengers speculated that this was due to the plentiful food available in America.

The quartermaster also explained that the frigate would travel 24 miles before reaching the open sea. After those introductions, the quartermaster proceeded to issue the daily rations. Hot water was soon available for tea and coffee and the families squatted on deck to eat their breakfast. For hours the ship followed the Maas River, its waters dark and languid. The older passengers were pensive while watching the countryside, knowing that they would never step their foot on Dutch soil again.

After crossing a large bay, the ship entered a canal through Voorne Island. Ropes were thrown to the shore and a team of horses pulled the ship along the canal. Late in the evening they reached the town of Hellevoetsluis where the captain anchored for the night in the harbor.

At early dawn, the sound of the crew preparing for departure woke the emigrants. Pushing in unison on the anchor windlass, the sailors were singing a sea shanty:

"Way, hay, up she rises,
Way, hay, up she rises,
Way, hay, up she rises,
Earlye in the morning! "

The quartermaster considered the cadenced refrain too repetitious. He started to sing the verses of the **Maid of Amsterdam** shanty and was soon joined by his mates:

"In Amsterdam there lived a maid
Mark you well what I say!
In Amsterdam there lives a maid,
And this fair maid my trust betrayed.

Then a great big Dutchman rammed my bow
Mark well what I do say
For a great big Dutchman rammed my bow,
And said, "Young man, dis bin mein vrow (wife)!"

The passengers understood only the last line and were intrigued by what the song was all about. The quartermaster grinned as he summarized the earlier lines sung in English, "The sea shanty you just heard states that it is dangerous for a sailor to pick up a girlfriend in a Dutch port. Her Dutch husband will seek a revenge on your ship."

Lifting his eyes to the open sea, the quartermaster continued, "All in all, we are fortunate to have favorable winds and fair weather. Sometimes ships have to anchor here for days or even weeks waiting for storms to subside. Take a last look at Holland because most likely you will never see it again. And consider yourself lucky because you are on the way to America, the land of freedom and prosperity for everybody."

The emigrants looked back at Hellevoetsluis, a typical small Dutch town with the windmills on the walls, and a church near the center of town. The sight of the church steeple left them with mixed feelings. Their dissent from the Reformed (State) Church was one of the major factors prompting them to leave Holland. While the town's church stood for oppression, it also represented stability. Their ship embodied a different contradiction: it was carrying them to wonderful prospects but also to a perilous and uncertain journey.

The brisk wind filled out the sails and the ship plowed

steadily through white-capped waves. Practically all the emigrants remained on deck watching the shores grow smaller. Along the way they sailed close to some fishing boats and the children waved and shouted greetings to the fishermen. One of the boats passed close to the ship and a fisherman tossed them a large cod. Scrambling, a small boy grabbed the fish from the deck and proudly presented it to his parents. It would be boiled and served to the family and their friends later that day.

The fish seemed to remind the quartermaster to issue the daily food and water rations to the passengers. He had to carefully weigh all the portions so it took an hour before all food was issued. Their first meal on the open sea was bread with cheese with hot tea or coffee for a drink. Right after they finished eating, the women formed a line to the cooking places to prepare hot meals for later during the day. There were only four cooking slots and nearly fifty families so even in good weather, most would not have a chance to prepare a hot meal everyday.

Most young passengers enjoyed the novelty of the sea journey. Jan Koeffers and his friends claimed one of the best locations near the bow of the ship. From there they watched the white spray as the ship plowed through the waves. They also eagerly scanned the horizon for more fishing boats. Late in the afternoon Jan was the first one to notice a school of dolphins approaching the ship. The graceful creatures leaped over the white-topped waves created by the bow of the ship. All boys were fascinated by those exuberant circus-like acts.

An older farmer standing near the boys was more interested in dolphins as potential fresh meat. "I sure hope that the sailors will catch one of those sea pigs. They don't seem to belong to anybody and I am curious how their meat will taste like."

Overhearing the remark, the quartermaster immediately

reprimanded the man. "It would be bad luck for the mariners to kill a dolphin. The graceful creatures are the favorites of Neptune, the god of the sea, and he would surely take a revenge on the whole ship."

The dolphins seemingly sensed the man's foul intentions and quickly departed. The boys soon stopped watching the sea and squatted down to exchange tales of the Indians and buffaloes roaming America.

The men remained standing about the deck in small groups, totally unaccustomed to being idle. Back home there was always something to do on their farms. They would also help their neighbors who were building a barn or a new home. Aboard the ship, however, all major tasks such as unfurling the sails and trimming the lines required experience and precise coordination. The stretches of frantic activity by the sailors were followed by periods of routine shipboard activities or ship watches.

The men could only discuss weather and compare their first journey impressions. As usual, they let the elders speak first. Teunis Koffers commented that so far the journey was not uncomfortable. They were warned about seasickness but on that first day all the passengers seemed to be all right.

The quartermaster spent most of his free time with the passengers, pleased to be able to converse in his native Dutch language. He readily proceeded with an explanation to the group as to what could be expected during their journey.

"We actually started out under perfect weather conditions. With more wind, the ship will be lifted by the big waves and then fall back down, like a child on a rocking board. With less wind, the ship will roll like a pig in a mud hole. I hope we will have a fast journey as it is my last cruise of the season. I am looking forward to see my wife and children soon."

Pointing to the dark clouds, he continued, "I prefer brisk winds or even stormy weather to the stretches of calm weather when the ship hardly moves for days."

The men asked the quartermaster how long he lived in America.

"More than twelve years. In 1832 I received a draft notice from the Dutch army. I knew I would be sent to fight the Belgian rebels and I just did not believe in killing fellow Christians. So I ran away, initially to England; later I signed up on an American ship. Ended up marrying a girl in New York of Dutch descent. They keep up the Dutch traditions but don't speak the language any more. In America people of Dutch descent have a reputation as hard working and prosperous."

The men continued with more questions, pressing him for information about Wisconsin and Michigan. The quartermaster replied that life in the New Territories was not for him.

"There are too many American pioneers and speculators moving west. They cut down trees, burn the logs, and grow wheat between the tree trunks still sticking out above the ground. After several seasons, yields go down and the Americans repeat the process at a new location."

The men pondered over this new information, shaking their heads. It was inconceivable for them to cultivate the land without first removing the tree trunks. Finally, Teunis Koffers stated the group's view about the American pioneer farmers.

"The speculators are simply poor farmers. Good farmers know that it is necessary to alternate the crops on the land to maintain good yields. Removing tree trunks is also a common sense necessity as it will simplify plowing and improve land utilization."

As evening came, it became clear that most families would not get their turn at the cooking slots. Many families shared their hot meals with their neighbors. Arrangements were made for the following day for families to combine their portions and cook them together. The emigrants remained in good spirits.

There was plenty of hot water for tea and coffee, the weather was fair, and they were making good progress.

By dusk, most families started to return to their bunks to avoid tripping in the dark. Some men remained on the top deck lured by the moon and the stars visible between the clouds. The weather was changing. As the night wore on, the wind slacked off with intermittent gusts and the ship began to roll heavily from side to side. In the darkness of the steerage compartment, a few children started to cry while others jeered them. The adults ordered the kids to hush but whispering continued across the compartment.

It wasn't long before the first person moaned that she was getting seasick. Her husband first chided her but then led her to the ladder and onto the deck. The woman started to throw up before she even reached the side of the ship.

"I'm sorry, " she said. "I guess I am just not made for traveling the oceans."

Her husband responded gruffly, "If you keep throwing up all your food, you are not going to survive this journey. Now get your mind set on what to feed your children tomorrow and forget that you are traveling on a ship."

Breathing heavily, the woman fought hard to restrain her queasy feeling and then started to sob.

The husband became more attentive, placed his arm around her shoulders, and whispered. "We are Dutchmen and our people sailed the seas before America was discovered. If the American sailors can take it, so can we. Before you know it, we will be in America and will be living on our own eighty acre farm."

During the night many other adults and children struggled up the ladder and to the side of the ship. Babies were crying while their mothers or older siblings tried to hug and comfort them. A few toddlers threw up over the side of their bunks or simply on the bedding.

A small boy whispered, "Please, can we return home."

The father whispered back, reciting the Lord's Prayer.

It was a long miserable night with people dozing and then waking up again. Lying awake, many wondered whether they had made the right decision to go to America. They had been warned that on a typical transatlantic crossing several passengers would die. Naturally they had assumed that it would be somebody else. At this point, a doubt started to grow in their minds whether they would survive the journey. They already felt wretched and they had not encountered any storms yet.

Eventually the wind picked up and the rolling of the ship decreased somewhat. The morning brought relief from the smelly stuffy steerage compartment as families spread out outside on the deck. For several days, good weather with steady winds prevailed. The coast was no longer in sight and only rarely a small ship could be spotted in the distance. The younger passengers continued to enjoy the daylight hours as long as it was not raining and they could stay on the top deck. The women remained busy by tending the children and planning and preparing the meals. Most passengers still felt queasy when returning to their smelly compartment at nightfall. After the first couple of nights, however, it was rare for anyone to get seasick.

The men grew restless by the inactivity and their lack of control over the developments around them. They held endless debates on the best farming methods for the new land. Wheat was the best cash crop but sometimes failed in years with drought. Farmers were advised to plant mostly Indian corn, which was easier to grow and produced good yields. That meant getting used to food made out of the corn flour and they were not sure they could subsist on such a strange diet.

Teunis Koffers wondered how much wooded acreage he

would be able to clear before the first planting season. He could not understand stories about the American settlers who simply cut and burned the trees and planted the wheat between the tree trunks. Wood was very valuable in Europe and it also sold for reasonable prices in America. Seeking out the quartermaster, Koeffers asked him why those settlers didn't sell the trees to sawmills or as firewood to the steamships?

The quartermaster shrugged, explaining that he had only a limited knowledge of the conditions in the New Territories.

"From what I have heard, the Yankees usually buy cheap land far away from the settlements and sawmills. Firewood can be sold to steamships but it takes time to cut the wood, followed by a long journey on bad trails to haul it to a nearby port. The Yankees say that it is easier to burn the trees, with ashes serving as fertilizer for the land. Some settlers are collecting ashes and selling them for as much as six cents a bushel."

The men shook their heads in disbelief. The trees on their farms would never be burned. Nor would they allow the tree trunks to remain forever in the soil. They were Dutchmen and nothing would be wasted or done improperly.

The first week aboard the ship went by quickly. The weather had been fair and they made good progress. They were far away from land now and days would pass without seeing another sail on the horizon. A lonely seagull remained with the ship and was befriended and fed by the children.

The steerage compartment remained stuffy and some passengers spent part of the night on deck. The skies were usually full of bright stars, thousands of them trying to outshine each other. On occasions, the ocean would also glow with such a luminous display that the ship seemed to glide through liquid fire.

During the day, the waves varied subtly in height and

appearance. On rare occasions a few flying fish would jump out of the water. One time the ship passed through a concentration of slimy-looking objects of various colors and forms, which stretched as far as one could see. More entertaining were the appearances of the *Portuguese men of war,* which rode on the crests of the rolling billows and stretched their tiny colorful sails as if trying to rise into the skies.

After ten days, the tranquility of the journey was shattered by several days of stormy weather and drenching cold rain. The steerage passengers had to remain in their compartment day and night, with all openings shut. The air was stale and there was a penetrating stench of vomit and human waste from the buckets. Some of the urine spilled and leaked into the bilge water, which sloshed below the decks.

For three days, they lived on bread and water only. It was impossible to boil water for tea or coffee and the raw water acquired a musty foul taste. Finally, the winds subsided sufficiently to make it safe for the passengers to get on the deck. Full food rations were drawn and fires started to boil water and make some hot food. It was still drizzling outside but the emigrants ventured out to breathe the fresh air. The children were most disappointed because their seagull could no longer be found anywhere on the ship.

Over the next several days the weather improved and skies turned from dark gray to blue, with an occasional parade of whimsical white clouds. It was the third week since leaving Rotterdam and many passengers expected that soon they would arrive in New York. The quartermaster's update was disappointing. The frigate was barely halfway across the Atlantic. With the winds growing lighter, the journey could take another three or four weeks.

Chapter 7

Crossing The Atlantic –
The Second Half

"Young America" by Richard C. Moore, www.shippainting.com

In the middle of the fourth week at sea, a surprising and welcome transformation took place. The foul drinking water became sweet again. At first only a few of the Dutch passengers commented on the difference while drinking their hot drinks. The taste improvement was most welcome. It was like a difference between water from a fresh stream and a stagnant pool. Still, the wary emigrants merely attributed it to their water rations being issued from a different cask.

When asked to comment on the water taste, the quartermaster provided an interesting explanation. "Normally as weeks pass, all water becomes foul and I have to add vinegar to make it bearable to drink. But sometime foul water mysteriously turns sweet on its own and a few days later changes back to foul. That's just the way it is, at least with some casks on some trips. You need to enjoy it while it lasts."

Young emigrants of the courting age were enjoying a different aspect of the journey. Fair weather meant that families spent most of their time on the main deck. Two couples could be seen openly spending time together. It was common knowledge that they would be getting married shortly after the group's arrival in the New Territories. For them, the journey provided a period of a prolonged though restrained courtship, with their parents never far away. Still, they spent more time together aboard the ship than they would back home where there were always chores to perform.

Even with everybody on the main deck, it was difficult for girls to make new acquaintances. Each family with daughters was also likely to have several sons. With no chores to perform, the boys spent their time screening their sisters' contacts. Suitors were expected to be from the same community and needed to gain the family's approval to court the daughter.

Bachelors strolled between the different passenger groups just to exchange glances with the maidens. A few bolder men would actually say some passing comments and try to make friends with the girls' brothers. Each day they spent more time with their new sweethearts. They talked about the future and even discussed how to persuade their families to end up in the same settlement. The customs of the day and the lack of privacy ensured, however, that the couples never kissed each other or even held their hands.

Perhaps the most closely chaperoned girl among the passengers was the pretty twenty-year old Hendrika Landeweerd. Her parents and three younger brothers all wanted to make sure that only proper suitors with good intentions could approach her. Her two married sisters and their husbands also acted as the guardians of the family honor. Hendrika kept busy looking after her three-year-old and fourteen-year-old sisters. She smiled to many men who had tried to court her but felt strangely attracted to one handsome stranger. She found from the other girls that his name was Derk Voskuil. It was a shame that he was from a different province and thus probably not acceptable to her parents.

Days passed. The weather remained fair and the wind was weak. Youngsters continued to find entertainment amid the shipboard life. Jan Koffers tried to learn English from the quartermaster whenever he was available. Soon he knew how to count and greet others. He proudly approached several sailors saying, "Hallo, my name is Jan and I am fifteen-years-old." To his greatest disappointment, the American sailors simply ignored him.

The quartermaster explained to Jan that his fellow sailors were rough men and had little patience for children. "But don't worry. In America, most people are generally friendly toward the Hollanders and often help and explain things to the foreign settlers in their area. If an American explains something to you, try your best to follow his advice and then show your appreciation. Americans like to be helpful. When they see that their assistance is appreciated, they will root for your success."

The quartermaster had more advice for Jan and his friends. "Each state and each community in America considers itself to be 'the home of the brave.' In most cases, such claims are backed by valiant deeds and intrepid spirit. A stranger adapting to the spirit of that phrase will be granted a quick acceptance."

When the quartermaster was busy, Jan and other children would sit for hours watching the ocean. Each hoped they would be the first to spot a passing ship and gain the prestige as the best lookout. One day Jan was surprised to hear a little boy exclaim, "Look, a sea monster is chasing us!"

Overhearing his cry, the nearby adults were startled. Other children quickly glanced across the sea and then scoffed at the boy. "It's all in his mind; he's heard too many stories about sea monsters."

Pointing, the boy told them to look at the sky. There, right above them, was a cloud resembling a huge whale with an enormous gaping mouth.

Children and adults raised their heads and stared at the cloud, hovering above them like a bad omen. Many children and adults immediately recalled all the previous dire forewarnings.

Jan's father, Teunis Koffers, was the first to break the spell. "This is just a cloud. From now on, anybody who mentions sea monsters again will get a thrashing. You children have been away from school for too long. Stop wasting your time looking at the clouds and start reciting your school verses and arithmetic tables."

The incident rekindled the passengers' hidden fears about the hazards present in the middle of the ocean. The young ruffians in Rotterdam were not the first ones to scare them with stories about sea monsters swallowing whole ships. They had previously read about many sailing ships disappearing without a trace during their journeys. One newspaper account described two ships sailing at night in fair weather. They were close to one another and the ship lights were clearly visible. Suddenly the lights of one ship simply disappeared. The sailors on watch swore that a monster swallowed the ship. The unfortunate ship was never heard of again.

Many emigrants had a premonition that the ocean would soon claim a victim. Still, nobody paid much attention when Jan Essenlinkpas first complained about stomach pains. The following day, he stayed the whole day in his bunk writhing in pain. There was no doctor aboard the ship and the quartermaster prepared some special brew for him to drink. Sometime during that night, he simply passed away. His brother Hendrik found it incomprehensible that Jan, aged only thirty-four, could pass away so quickly.

Turning to his sister-in-law, Hendrik declared, "I will help you to build a cabin in Wisconsin. You can also count on me to help you to raise my brother's five children."

A secret doubt was gnawing in Hendrik's mind, "Would Jan be still alive, if they had all remained in Holland?"

Jan's burial at sea was short and simple. The captain said a prayer in English and the body, sewn in a canvas bag, was sent sliding into the water. Watching the waves that had swallowed the body bag, the Hollanders seemed stunned. Nobody spoke, awaiting a eulogy that they normally would hear from a minister at home.

An awkward minute passed and Gerrit Geerlings realized that he was the only person there with a background as a deacon. He did not know the deceased man and had only spoken a few times with the men from Essenlinkpas's Winterswijk group. Nonetheless he knew that it was his obligation to address the grieving passengers.

Looking at the somber faces around him, Geerlings began, "The Lord moves in mysterious ways...."

His voice was strong yet soothing. The Hollanders turned toward him and awaited his explanation of the tragedy. "The main reason we are taking this journey is to acquire the freedom to properly worship our Lord. What possible reason could there be for Lord to take one of our brothers before we even get to our destination? Could it be a sign that we have made a wrong decision, that the new world will corrupt and deprave us? Or is it the Lord's punishment because we have left our kin, or in some cases even our parents, behind us?"

Geerlings paused, letting the listeners gather their own reflections. After a moment he resumed by reciting the highlights of Dutch history as well as the tribulations suffered by their nation. The Dutch people had converted the wave-swept wilderness into Europe's most fertile country. Every century, however, there was a terrible price to be paid when great storms would breach the dikes and drown thousands of people. The Hollanders had also had to face and overcome their jealous enemies who started wars and, at times, occupied and plundered their homes.

"God has tested our people many times. Thanks to our Lord, we, the survivors, are invincible in spirit and able to face any challenge in the world. The Lord does move in mysterious ways. We must trust his judgment as to why our brother Jan Essenlinkpas had to leave us so prematurely. All our ordeals will only strengthen the resolve of those chosen by the Lord to spread his glory in this new Promised Land."

The eulogy provided a needed closure to the ceremony. Afterwards, a ring of men formed around Geerlings, eager to persuade him to become a deacon in their new settlement. Teunis Koffers stated that his group needed Geerlings' spiritual guidance and that they would build a home for him and his family.

Geerlings pondered the prospect before replying. "The first snow will come in Wisconsin before anybody finishes even a simple shelter. My family must spend the winter in Milwaukee or I fear that my wife might not survive. Perhaps next year, when your colony gets established, there will be time to build a church and a deacon's home. Perhaps we will also be able to build a flour mill so I can serve both as a deacon and a miller, as I have done in the past...."

The men were disappointed that Geerlings would not spend the first winter with them. At the same time they were encouraged by the indication that he was considering joining them the following year.

Meanwhile, the women comforted Jan's widow and children. Hendrik Essenlinkpas, the bachelor brother-in-law, solemnly renewed his promise to help build a cabin and clear the land. Other men approached the widow and also offered help. The wife was weeping and did not respond, still unable to comprehend the future without her husband.

Out of respect, the quartermaster waited for half an hour before he started to issue the daily food and water rations. Most passengers spent the rest of the day wondering how many more victims would be claimed. On most transatlantic crossings, several passengers would die from sickness or accidents. Essenlinkpas was a strong healthy man. Since he died so quickly, it could be anybody's turn next.

The emigrants stayed on deck the rest of the day. In the evening, the sun turned red as it approached the horizon. Somebody started softly singing a hymn about the Lord, the protector of the mariners. Others joined, also in low, poignant voices. More religious psalms followed while the crimson sun slowly sank below the water. The sky in the west remained orange and it took a long time before dusk and darkness finally prevailed.

Approaching the group, the ship's quartermaster spoke softly. "I am sorry about Jan Essenlinkpas. Still, I am fairly sure that his sickness was not connected to the ship. He would have ended up the same way, even if he were back on his farm."

There was no reply. The men in the group were lost in their

private thoughts. The quartermaster decided they needed to be distracted and recited a popular sailor's verse.

"Red sky at night, sailor's delight;
Red sky at morning, sailor take warning."

He followed with the explanation that the red sunset they had just witnessed meant good weather for the following day.

"Enjoy it while it lasts. I just hope that the winds will pick up soon. This is shaping up to be one my slowest transatlantic crossings."

A whole week passed with beautiful red sunsets as the wind grew slacker with each day. They reached the point when the sails stayed limp for hours at a time while the waters around them were still as in a pond. For several days they didn't seem to move at all. The sky was cloudless and the sun was overpowering so one had to squint just to view the horizon. At night, the skies were filled with thousands of stars, a lot more than they could ever see in the usually cloudy skies of Holland. The bright moon casted a silvery road on the surface of the ocean, as if trying to lure the travelers to step off the ship and walk to their destination.

One of the passengers recalled a story from a newspaper about a sailing ship that became stranded for months in becalmed waters. It finally reached land after six months, with most of the passengers and crew dead. The men sought out the quartermaster to seek his opinion about such a possibility.

"Nay, that's impossible. Perhaps, they got blown off the trade-wind route and got stuck somewhere in the tropics. You men don't have to worry about our ship being stuck here for months. Captain Meyers knows what he is doing and those stretches of no-wind never last more than a week in the North Atlantic. In the years I've been crossing this ocean, the slowest journey that I can recall lasted less than nine weeks."

The next day there was a sense of a change in the air. At dawn, clouds were visible in the sky and weak gusts of wind intermittently filled the sails. The ship was moving and the bow was forming small waves. The mood of despair was quickly replaced by renewed optimism.

The following morning, a red sun appeared above the water. The sails were billowing in the wind and white foam appeared as the ship's bow sliced through the water. The ship was traveling at a good pace and nobody minded when later that afternoon they got hit by a rainsquall. Most of the passengers remained on deck, savoring the initial refreshing drizzle. Soon the drizzle turned into a heavy rain. The hatches were closed and the air in the compartment started to turn humid and rank. At this point, the passengers were willing to accept this condition as long as it meant speeding up their arrival in America.

Several days of gray skies and intermittent rain followed. A few times, they saw sails of another ship far in the distance. The passengers took it as a sign they were getting close to America and that they would be helped even if their ship were to get in trouble. It was eight weeks since the departure from Holland and they were anxious to stand on firm ground. Two days later, they could see sails almost in every direction, with some small fishing boats passing close enough for crewmen to talk to fishermen and confirm their position. Soon after that, the ship changed course on a more southerly direction. They were within three or four days of reaching New York.

A new sense of excitement and determination spread among the passengers. There would be no more victims. They could survive three days even if all the food and water were to disappear. If their ship were to sink, they still would have a chance to float to land on makeshift rafts. The Lord was bringing them to the Promised Land.

The lookout's first glimpse of land was late at night. A few emigrants were still on deck and they quickly roused the rest of the passengers. Only a few mothers with small children remained in their bunks while everybody else climbed to the top deck. It was a dark night, with no stars overhead, and they could barely see the outline of land. The sails were trimmed and the ship made little headway through the rest of the night. Passengers recited prayers of thanks and then talked excitedly about what would be their first meal on land.

Jan Koeffers knew well what he would choose, "Ah, a rich chicken stew with a big slice of fresh dark bread."

In daylight, they could see that they were traveling in a large bay. The quartermaster explained that the mainland was on the right while on the left was Long Island. They were surprised to see big patches of woods with few homes and no windmills. Compared to Holland, this was wilderness, even though they were close to a large city.

The quartermaster issued the last food rations. He also instructed the passengers to empty their mattresses and throw the straw overboard. Soon the water behind the ship formed a wide straw-covered path. Ahead of them the passengers could see the first structures of New York and dozens of small and large sails everywhere. A steamship passed them and loudly blew its horn, scaring the children and adults alike.

Smiling, the quartermaster chided his passengers.

"That steamship has just welcomed you to America. Congratulations, you have survived the transatlantic journey."

Chapter 8

New York – Hudson River

New York, Magasin pittoresque, 1858

After a journey of 61 days, the frigate *France* arrived in New York on Tuesday, October 26th, 1847. Ahead of them, the passengers observed with amazement a forest of tall chimneys spewing plumes of smoke into the sky. Huge warehouses lined the waterfront; beyond them were rows after rows of even taller buildings. The ship's quartermaster proudly explained that nearly half a million people lived in New York, five times more than in Rotterdam. Jan Koeffers boldly replied that the largest city in the world was London with a population of over two million people.

Before the ship was allowed to dock, the passengers first had to pass a medical examination. The doctor who came aboard was pleased to hear that only one passenger had died during the transatlantic passage. The frigate was a reputable American ship and the passengers were almost all Dutch. There was no reason to suspect that the cursed "ship fever" had plagued this vessel and thus no need for thorough examinations. He walked past the rows of mostly ruddy-cheeked Dutch passengers, briefly inspecting those who seemed pale or worn out by the journey.

All around them were dozens of anchored sailing ships. The doctor explained, "Those ships are full of Irish passengers and will remain in quarantine for weeks. New York is simply overwhelmed with sick immigrants and nobody suspected of ship fever is allowed to reach shore. However, we have an American frigate here and all the passengers are Dutch or German so the quarantine will not be necessary."

The ship was cleared to proceed to the pier where the immigration agent started to compile the passengers' list. The immigration records registered the passengers' names, their ages, occupation, country of origin, and the amount of dollars they were bringing with them. The quartermaster assisted in translating the questions and answers.

The immigration agent performed an additional role to encourage the passengers to move directly to the inland destinations, without stepping foot in New York. The city was full of sick and jobless immigrants. The agent was happy to hear that a majority of the Dutchmen were planning to continue their journey to the New Territories by Lake Michigan. He then told the passengers to remain aboard and await a representative from the newly formed Dutch agency. The Dutch agent would help them with further tickets and travel arrangements.

The two German families traveling aboard the frigate declared that they would be stopping in New York to rest before resuming their journey. Also staying in New York were the two

Loume brothers from the Zeeland province, their wives and seven children. They had spent all their money on the ship passage and needed to find work before they would travel any farther. Several unmarried young Dutch passengers were also short on money and chose to find jobs in New York.

Right from start, the Seceder families had vowed to travel together to the New Territories around Lake Michigan. Hendrik Wilterdink was greatly surprised when his brother Jan announced that he was planning to stay behind in New York with his wife. Hendrik knew that Jan did not have much money and assured him again that he would help them with the land purchase and the expenses.

Jan Wilterdink merely shook his head. "The reason we want to stay in New York is because of my wife's pregnancy. By the time we get to Wisconsin, there will be snow on the ground and it will take weeks to build a cabin. I will get a job in New York and we will spend the winter here. You, my brother, buy as much land in Wisconsin as you can. We will earn some money here and join you next spring."

Hendrik reminded his brother that they had agreed to travel and start the new farmsteads together but Jan was adamant.

"The journey across the Atlantic took weeks longer than a typical voyage. Our cousin Herman is also staying with us in New York. His mother is seventy years old and would not survive nights in the snow while we are building a cabin. We will stay together in New York and earn money to help with next year's farm expenses."

An hour after the ship docked, a Dutch-speaking agent of the recently formed "Netherlands Society for the Protection of the Emigrants from Holland" came aboard. The agent warned the passengers that as soon as they would step ashore, they would be harassed or possibly robbed. Sometimes small children were forcefully carried away and returned only when their parents agreed to stay at some rundown hotel with exorbitant prices.

The Netherlands Society, supported by the existing Dutch community in New York, offered free or low cost lodging accommodations to those who wanted to remain in New York. For passengers continuing their travel to the New Territories, the Society arranged reasonably priced meals and organized further transportation. Those traveling to Wisconsin first had to take a steamship and spend a day traveling up the Hudson River to Albany. The safest and most convenient way to transfer to the new ship would be by boats.

For weeks, the passengers had been looking forward to the day they would reach land and be able to walk on firm ground. The families bound for the New Territories were disappointed that they would not even step a foot in New York. At the same time, from the deck of their ship, they could see city hustlers and food vendors shouting and accosting anybody in sight. It was best to let the Dutch agent handle all their arrangements.

The first priority was freshly cooked food. Since the majority of the passengers would not go ashore, instructions were sent to bring meals aboard. Shortly after the immigration processing had been completed, a horse cart arrived with several large pots of soups and stews, as well as pans of roasted chicken, mashed potatoes, vegetables, fresh bread, fruit, and pudding for dessert. For passengers, it was a feast surpassing any holiday meal in their memory.

The passengers lined up with their metal dishes while the cook and the Dutch agent dished out the various servings. Children at first accepted only two or three items and walked away. After all, even on a holiday or at a wedding it would be impolite for a child guest to eat too much.

The Dutch agent encouraged everybody to eat more. "The food in America is not expensive and will be equally paid for

by everybody. There are no additional charges for extra helpings
and all food should be finished off. You have just spent two
months at sea on an awful diet. You need fresh-cooked food to
recover strength for continuing their journey."

The children thoroughly enjoyed eating as much as they
wanted and then coming back for more fruit and pudding. The
sweet plums in Rotterdam were very special but the American
fruit was a lot more exotic. For the first time in their life, the children tasted oranges and bananas. The Dutch agent was amused,
watching a boy bite a banana complete with the skin.
Demonstrating how to skin the banana, the agent told the boys
that, in New York, they could eat a banana or orange every day!

Despite the agent's demonstration on how to peel the
banana, some adult Hollanders continued to eat skin and all.
One man grumbled, "Only the dainty city dwellers peel apples
or other fruit before eating them. Country folk eat their fruit
unpeeled. I certainly won't peel something as exotic as bananas."

While the passengers were finishing their meal, three
sloops, small sailing ships with a single mast, arrived by the
frigate. Soon the passengers started to transfer their baggage.
Afterwards, they said their final good byes to the quartermaster and waived to the rest of the crew. They were good men and
they had carried them safely across the Atlantic.

On route to their Hudson River steamship, the Hollanders
watched with amazement the tall masts of hundreds of ships
and boats and the hustle of the busy city. Beyond the rows of
the wharf warehouses were even taller buildings that surpassed
anything they had seen in Rotterdam. The city was fascinating but too hectic. The Dutch farmers wanted to get as quickly
to their future settlements as possible. A stopover in New York
would have been frivolous.

The agent from the Netherlands Society accompanied the
passengers on one of the sloops. He confirmed that life in New

York was rough for foreigners. There were a lot of gangs in the city who controlled jobs and demanded kickbacks and protection money. The city was full of Irish immigrants who had the advantage of speaking English.

Life in the New Territories was easier and the people there more tolerant. A lot of Germans had settled in Wisconsin, making it possible for most Hollanders to communicate with them. On the way to the New Territories, there were many cities with people of Dutch descent. At their first stopover in Albany, there was a Dutch-speaking minister Wyckoff. The Dutch agent gave the passengers the minister's address and encouraged them to contact him. Wyckoff would help with further travel arrangements and see to it that the travelers were not overcharged.

Before long, the sloops approached the steamship, which would take the Hollanders up the Hudson River. The ship was most impressive and even bigger that the frigate that took them across the Atlantic! Instead of masts it had two tall smokestacks. Above the deck was a huge palace-like structure, complete with dozens and dozens of windows. A great paddle side-wheel was sticking out of the water, somewhat reminding them of the Dutch windmills. It was hard to believe that it would cost only one dollar per person to travel on such a magnificent vessel.

The reason for the low cost of the tickets became clear once they were taken to their new accommodations. The steerage compartment on the steamship was just as crowded as the one on their transatlantic journey. Furthermore, there was only a small section on deck where they were allowed to come up for fresh air. They had to bring their own bread and provisions, arranged for them through the Netherlands Society agent. The steerage passengers were not welcome in the dining room of the cabin passengers.

Jan Koeffers commented that the one-dollar steamship ticket

for the one-day trip was actually expensive. The two-months transatlantic passage was fourteen dollars per person or about twenty-five cents a day. The sailing ships did not pay for fuel and thus were cheaper.

Derk Voskuil corrected Jan. "Most sailing ships cross the Atlantic in four to six weeks so fourteen dollars equals nearly fifty cents a day. The ticket for the steamship passage on the Great Lakes is five dollars or about eighty cents per day. But you must remember that the steamships travel twice as fast as the sailing ships and are safer in bad weather. The future belongs to steamships and, one day, they will replace sailing ships even on the transatlantic routes."

The following morning, dark smoke was rising from the smokestacks when the first of the Hollanders climbed up on deck. Additional passengers were still coming aboard and soon their steerage compartment section was packed. Just before nine o'clock, the deep steam whistle sounded twice and a few minutes later the ship departed.

The steamship was moving fast and New York's profile quickly receded beyond them. It was amazing how quickly the shores changed into wilderness. Hardly any dwellings were visible and tall trees grew among the rocky tall banks. By the time the passengers turned around to take one more look at New York, it was no longer in sight. Less than twenty miles from the city, they passed by the sheer basalt walls of the New Jersey Palisades. The riverbank was many times taller than the three-story high building in Rotterdam! The Hudson River, nearly a mile wide, was taking them into the increasingly deeper valley of wilderness.

A German-speaking sailor joined the steerage passengers to find out where they were from. They, in turn, peppered him with questions about the Hudson River and what was ahead of them. One of the elders did the translation while others eagerly listened.

"Our steamboat will travel one hundred forty miles from New York to Albany. The Hudson River is really like a Norwegian fiord: a wide, almost straight channel, with ocean tides surging through its deep waters as far inland as Albany. Soon you will see that the river will temporarily widen into the Tappan Zee, a fourteen-mile long stretch over two miles wide. After that, Hudson becomes narrower again and will weave through granite hills and mountains, rising as high as fifteen hundred feet right beside the river. During the revolution, heavy chains were stretched across the river to block the British fleet. Above the river were forts to guard the chains. Later today, you will be able to see one of those forts, West Point, which is now the site of the US Army military academy."

The passengers would not let the sailor leave. The name Tappan Zee was most intriguing. Zee meant "sea" in Dutch but the name Tappan was unrecognizable, though vaguely familiar.

Grinning, the sailor explained the meaning of the name. "Tappan Zee was an Indian-Dutch name meaning the 'cold stream sea.' The first white settlers in this area were Dutch, back in the early 1600s when New Amsterdam was under Dutch colonial rule. In 1664, after a naval blockade, the English took over and changed the name of the city and the state to New York. The mountains in this area still carry the old Dutch names. Dutch settlers also created legends about malicious mountain spirits to explain the frequent storms and the wicked river currents. But don't worry. We live in the 1840s now and you are traveling on the most modern steamboat on this river."

Perhaps they would have been better off not hearing those reassuring explanations from the German-speaking sailor. Soon the overwhelming, almost perpendicular granite mountains were towering right above the river. The sights filled the Hollanders with awe and terror as the cliffs seemed ready to collapse at any moment. In a storm, wouldn't a cascade of rocks and mountain slides fill the river and bury their ship? As they were passing one towering mountain, a howling wind hit the ship and the white-capped river currents pounded the ship. Wicked eddy currents were swirling all around the hull. Gradually the sudden fury subsided; the cliffs remained intact but still threatening.

Sometime later, the river took a sharp v-like turn and they passed above cliffs topped by tall buildings. Children recalled the sailor's story about the West Point fort guarding the chains stretched across the river. They sought out the German-speaking sailor to tell them more about the battles that occurred at this point.

The sailor's answer was most disappointing. "The British considered this strongpoint to be impregnable. Their fleet did not even attempt to force their way past West Point."

Soon it turned dark and the passengers finally retired to their compartment. The memories of the mountains were still fresh in their minds and they wondered what was lying ahead of them. In their letters, the pioneers had described Wisconsin and Michigan as a fairly flat country and made no mention of any nearby mountains. How could one cultivate land surrounded by granite hills?

The following morning the river continued its course, deep at the bottom of a valley, but the riverbanks were not as steep or overhanging. Every so often the steamboat passed small communities located just above the river. The Hudson River still remained about a mile wide and because of this it was difficult to spot people on the banks. Soon, they saw a large city on the horizon. The German-speaking sailor passed by and told the Hollanders that in less than an hour they would reach Albany.

Chapter 9

Albany – Erie Canal

Albany, Illustrated London News, 1846

Albany was located near the end of the navigable portion of the spectacular Hudson River. Along the way, the steamboat passengers had traveled over one hundred miles through the towering mountains and wilderness. At the end of the river journey, the sight of this large city of fifty thousand people was astonishing, like a mirage in a desert. Amazingly, Albany was the oldest European settlement in the state, dating back to 1614, and was the capital of the New York State. Many city notables were descendents of the original Dutch Indian traders and pioneers. President Martin Van Buren, who led the country between 1836 and 1840, was of Dutch descent. In the twentieth century, two more famous New Yorkers of Dutch descent,

Theodore Roosevelt and Franklin Roosevelt, would become great Presidents.

Albany was spread out on a sloped terrain above the river, with major streets leading right to the ship landings. The Hudson River was about a mile wide at this point, with rows of barges tied up along the shores. Additional "line boats" were floating on the river, fastened to the sides of the steam tow-boats. Most of those barges were delivering wheat flour from the Erie Canal communities to the voracious New York.

A crowd of peddlers gathered at the ship landing as soon as they heard the steam whistle of the big steamship. The passengers, coming down the gangplank, were steered to a particular hotel or were offered tickets and assistance to the trains.

After all cabin passengers had disembarked, the steerage passengers were finally allowed to disembark the steamboat. Warily, the Dutch immigrants carried their baggage and held on to their children. They remembered the warnings about the New York hustlers stealing bags or holding children for ransom. A number of pushy men milled around the group, shouting something incomprehensible in English. The immigrants formed a circle and hoped they would be able to quickly contact their Dutch-speaking host.

A young man was nominated for the task of finding the Dutch minister Wyckoff. With the minister's address written on a piece of paper, the man eventually located his home. Within an hour, both men returned to the Dutch passengers. The minister was an older bearded man wearing a dark suit and clearly was eager to help them. Greetings were exchanged and the men answered the minister's questions about Dutch provinces they had come from.

The minister then queried the travelers about their destinations. "Are you traveling to join Reverend Van Raalte in

Michigan? I have received letters stating that their settlement is progressing well."

Gerrit Geerlings replied for the group, "Some of us are heading for the Van Raalte's colony but the majority will probably settle in Wisconsin. We would appreciate it if you could advise us about the best destinations. A few of our families are also considering joining the Dutch settlers in Iowa."

The minister found it amazing that, after traveling thousands of miles, some immigrant families still had not chosen a firm destination.

"Well, you certainly don't want to buy a farm here, as some farmland near Albany sells for over one hundred dollars an acre. In the New Territories, I would avoid moving to Iowa. The virgin prairie land there is tough and a lot of money is needed to develop a profitable farm. I receive only positive reports about the Michigan Dutch settlement. Their only drawback is the inflated land cost set by the area speculators. The best prospects for a large group are in Wisconsin. Make sure that you have enough money to live until the first harvest. If you are short on cash, you should stay in New York State and work here through the winter."

The Hollanders were anxious to buy land and spend the winter cutting trees and preparing for the spring planting. It was crucial to continue their journey without interruptions. Geerlings asked for the minister's view on the transportation options, "What is the best way to travel to Buffalo: by train or by barge on the Erie Canal?"

Minister Wyckoff patiently provided a detailed comparison.

"Most Americans travel to Buffalo by train because it's faster and costs the same as the barge: five dollars per person. However, traveling by train, you will have to pay extra for your sea chests. Furthermore, trains can be dangerous. Occasionally they don't follow timetables and two trains will crash into each other. There are also accidents because the wooden rails are covered with flimsy strips of iron. With the train speeding, the strapping sometimes springs up, slashing and killing the passengers in a coach. The barges, on the other hand, are slow and quite dirty. You are likely to catch lice and get bitten by bed bugs at night. However, Dutch people are used to barges and most of them choose to travel by the Erie Canal."

A few of the passengers refused to even consider traveling by train, often said to be the creation of the devil. The group did not want to separate and chose to travel together by the Erie Canal.

Listening to their discussion, the minister shook his head. "There are too many of you to travel together on one barge. The passenger barges, called packet boats, can carry close to a hundred passengers but in very crowded conditions. Usually half of the passengers sleep in the bunks while others sleep one next to another on the floor or on top of the tables. Also note that the Erie Canal passenger packet boats do not actually depart from Albany. The packet-boat passengers have to travel twenty miles by train to Schenectady from where the morning and evening boats depart for Buffalo."

The Hollanders were dismayed by the complicated arrangements and the need to haul their heavy baggage between multiple transfer points. They eagerly listened while the minister described an alternative arrangement.

"Direct travel from Albany to Buffalo is available on the combination cargo-passenger barges, called 'line boats.' The first day and a half will be spent just to reach nearby Schenectady in the Mohawk River Valley. During that first thirty miles, the line boats will travel through some twenty locks and will be raised over two hundred feet. The additional week and a half will be spent traveling the 333 miles from Schenectady to Buffalo. The line boats generally travel only during the day and thus are slower than the passenger pocket boats which never stop."

The Hollanders were more concerned about the ticket cost than the extra days of travel. Once again minister Wyckoff proceeded with the details for the travel and food expenses.

"The passenger packet boats have a fixed fare of 1.5 cents a mile including food, which is mostly bread with fried cutlets or fish. A passenger will thus pay $5 from Schenectady to Buffalo plus the train fare from Albany to Schenectady. The ticket and food costs on the line boats are negotiable but competitive with the packet boats. The line boats allow more baggage and will charge six or seven dollars."

The minister knew that the Hollanders did not speak English and were hardly in a position to negotiate. They trusted him and would do whatever he recommended.

"I will have to leave you now to start making the travel and food arrangements. I will order hot food for the whole group and then check out how many line boats are available for tomorrow's departure. Hopefully most of you will be able to spend the night aboard the line boats, each of which will take around forty passengers."

An hour and half later the minister returned. He had completed arrangements for three line boats to pick up the Dutch passengers and depart the next morning. The one hundred twenty passengers were able to move their baggage directly to their boats. The rest of the travelers could travel by train to Schenectady and catch the evening passenger packet boat or a train from there. Or the minister would find them sleeping quarters in Albany and they would start their journey the following day.

The Hollanders held a conference on who would travel on the three line boats. They also agreed that the Buffalo's waterfront would be their assembly place so they could travel together on the same steamship. The line boats leaving the next morning were expected to reach Buffalo by November 10th. Priorities for boarding those boats were given to the largest group from Winterswijk plus those with a lot of baggage. Everyone else chose to stay overnight in Albany trusting Wyckoff to make the best arrangements.

The line boat travelers proceeded to move their baggage to their new quarters. The line boats were seventy-five feet long and twelve feet wide. Two large cabins were located forward and aft, with an open middle section where freight was carried. The passenger space was even more crowded than the steerage compartments on the previous ships. The stuffy, dimly lit cabins had wooden benches along the sides. The seats were so limited that most passengers would have to stand or sit on the floor. There seemed to be no provisions for sleeping accommodations. The sea chests and large baggage pieces were stored outside on deck.

Soon after the baggage had been stowed away, a horse cart arrived with the hot food ordered by the minister. There were a number of roasted chickens along with tubs of potatoes and soup. There was plenty of fresh bread and butter, as well as apples and pears.

A small boy complained, "Our dinner in New York was better because they had oranges there."

Minister Wyckoff scoffed. "When you visit New York again, you will eat oranges which are inexpensive there. In Albany and in the New Territories, we eat local food and fruit. In any case, our pears are sweeter than any oranges."

Back in Holland, a meal on most days meant bread usually without butter. On other days, potatoes were served along with vegetable soup where tiny bits of bacon would be savored as a great prize. If a chicken was offered, it generally meant that either the recipient or the chicken were sick.

What they had here was a feast: roasted chicken, soup, potatoes with gravy, and fresh bread with butter! The elders knew that during their first winter in Wisconsin food would be scarce again. They were still recovering from the rough voyage across the Atlantic and needed to gain strength for what was ahead of them. Another fifteen hundred miles of journey remained, to be followed by weeks of living in the cold while cabins were built.

While the passengers ate, the line boat crew set up two rows of sleeping bunks, set up above the wooden benches. Narrow canvas-covered wooden frames were fastened to the ceiling on one side. The protruding ends on the other side of the frames were pushed into the holes in the wall. Fewer than half of the passengers could sleep in bunks. The rest would have to lay, one next to another, on the floor or on the tables.

Minister Wyckoff remained with the group until they had paid their fares and selected their sleeping accommodations. They were very crowded but at least had a place to stay for the night and would get to Buffalo with no more baggage transfers.

Before departing, Wyckoff passed on a final important safety instruction. During their trip, the line boats would pass under a number of very low bridges. The passengers were to be on alert and drop low on deck whenever they would hear a crewman blow a horn and shout in English "bridge" or "low bridge, everybody down."

The minister continued, "The cabins are crowded and there is not much room on the main deck. Some passengers will climb on top of the cabin from where there is a great view of the countryside. Being on the roof can be dangerous, however, because there is not much clearance between the top of the boat and most bridges. The canal folks often tell the story of a woman who fell asleep with her head on a box. Her head was crushed when the barge passed under a low bridge."

Soon it was dark and everybody settled for the night. The elders had the first choice on the bunks and found them very uncomfortable. There was very little space between the two rows of bunks and the canvas bottoms were sagging. It was impossible to turn without bumping those below. The passengers were issued only tiny pillows, not much bigger than a woman's handbag. The windows were closed due to the cold temperatures and soon it became extremely stuffy. There were only a few complaints since the Hollanders had already spent two months in similar conditions. At least nobody was going to get seasick while traveling in the canal boat.

Many men lay awake wondering about the next portion of their journey. The Hollanders were eager to see the cultivated land along the Erie Canal and observe American farming practices. The shipping agent back home had told them that forests covered most of eastern America before the arrival of the Europeans. The farms here could serve as a model for what their forested tracts in Wisconsin would eventually look like.

Less than three weeks of travel remained. The week and a half they would spend on the Erie Canal was bound to be very leisurely. After reaching Buffalo, they would travel for one week on a steamship. The Great Lakes were said to be quite stormy in November but comfort was of little concern to the emigrants. The Hollanders were anxious to reach their destinations, build shelter before the first snow, and start preparing the land for spring planting.

Chapter 10

Up the Mohawk River Valley

"Marco Paul's Travels on the Erie Canal"
by Heart of the Lakes Publishing

Early in the morning on Friday, October 29th, a well-dressed man in his early thirties came aboard the line boat. The boat captain greeted the passenger with deference and helped him store his baggage in the forward cabin, right next to his own quarters. Both men then returned to the deck and the crewmen cast off the lines. The eleven-day Erie Canal journey was about to begin.

The newly arrived gentleman walked up toward the group of Dutch passengers. He was friendly and not put off by the men's long beards and their disheveled appearance from the long journey.

"Welcome to America, my name is David Blish." Hearing no response, Blish tried to find out what country they were from. "Deutschland - Germany?"

Teunis Koffer finally replied in Dutch that they were from the Netherlands. His fifteen-year old son Jan collected enough courage to repeat the few English phrases he had learned during the transatlantic passage.

"My name is Jan Koffer. I come from Holland. I speak little English. I go to Wisconsin, the home of the brave."

Mister Blish grinned, watching the boy struggle as he recited the English words. He then pointed a finger to himself. "Wisconsin. I'm also going to Wisconsin. We will be traveling together. I have hardware merchandise aboard this boat. When we get to Buffalo, your men can help me transfer my merchandise to the steamship. I will help you earn your first money in America."

The only part the boy understood was that the man was also going to Wisconsin. "I go to Wisconsin. You go to Wisconsin, the home of the brave, ja?"

Blish nodded his head. "Ja, we will go to Wisconsin together. We can use brave lads like you in our state. There is plenty of time until we get there and I will teach you to speak more English."

In the meantime, the four crewmen: captain, bowsman, helmsman, and cook, were busy maneuvering the line boat with long poles. After twenty minutes, the boat reached the first lock. They were leaving the Hudson River behind them, which at this point, was still only one foot above the ocean level.

Slowly, the huge lock gates started to close. A deep shadow descended over the boat which was surrounded on all sides by towering stonewalls. Small children screamed as the onrushing turbulent water started to rock the boat and slowly lifted them upward. Long minutes passed before they finally approached the top of the lock and the water turbulence subsided. At last, with straining noises, the forward gates started to open.

The first lock raised the boat seven feet higher. After passing through a short canal, the line boat entered a second lock. This time, the water rising sequence was less scary since the passengers knew what to expect. Eventually, the forward gate opened and the boat was pushed out into a small basin.

Instead of proceeding on their journey, the boat was maneuvered into a strange third lock covered by a roof. All passengers had to step ashore. Next the water was drawn off and the boat ended up resting on a frame. The lockmaster measured the weight of the boat and compared it to the records showing the weight of the empty boat. The boat master then had to pay a toll for the freight and for each passenger.

Finally, the line boat was allowed to proceed to the canal. A young man, not older than eighteen, waved to the crew and quickly fastened the lines from the boat to the horses. Swearing, he spurred the horses, which strained forward while the boat slowly began to gather speed. After a couple of minutes the line boat reached a steady pace of about four miles an hour. The sullen young man walked on the towpath right behind the horses. He never looked back and only the taut towlines indicated that the line boat was following behind without any problems.

For ten miles they would travel parallel to the Hudson River. On their left they could see distant towering ridges covered with forests. On their right was the mile-wide Hudson River flowing just below them and the banks of the other shore.

The canal was very wide in this section. At first a lot of barges were tied up on the other side; some were even fastened in a tier to each other. Soon they came across the first barge coming toward them. The passengers were very curious to see the routine of how the line boats would pass each other. They were surprised to see the horses towing their boat continuing at the normal speed as if unaware of the horses approaching from the other direction.

At the last moment, the young man steered the horses to the edge of the towpath away from the canal. The horses stopped and the towline dropped to the ground allowing the other set of horses to pass over them. Shortly after that the helmsman steered the boat away from the towpath while the approaching boat steered toward the towpath. At that point, the horses stopped again allowing the towline to drop into the water and pass below the oncoming line boat. The whole operation was performed so smoothly that the boat hardly lost any speed.

Blish complimented the captain on the crew's skillful handling of the boat passing routine. If the towline had failed to pass below the boat, it could have swept the people off the line boat and dragged the horses into the water. How was it possible to train young men to lead the horses without making costly mistakes?

The captain smiled. "Ah, the young apprentices do make mistakes. But that's why the canal boats have a hooked knife attached to the bow. If the towline of the boat traveling in the opposite direction were to pass above rather than below the boat, the knife would cut it. After the novices have repaired the line once or twice, they quickly learn not to make the timing mistake again. Remember that we will pass hundreds of line and pocket boats before we get to Buffalo."

As time passed, some of the passengers went down to the cabin. Children congregated around Blish, chattering in Dutch.

Blish waved his hand to hush them and told them that in America they had to learn to speak English. He then raised his fingers and started to count in English. Soon a crowd of Dutch children and adults gathered around and repeated: one, two, three, four.... The lessons were not one sided. Blish in turn learned how to count in Dutch.

Afterwards Blish used hand gestures to explain other English words. Tree: he pointed to a nearby tree and also formed a tree trunk with one hand and branches with the other hand. Home: again he pointed to a dwelling while drawing the outline of building and roof with his other hand. Horse: he pointed to the two horses ahead of them and then pretended to be pulling the towline while neighing at the same time. The children laughed and repeated in English each phrase.

At the end of the lesson, they had an animated conversation about their journey in America. Blish started by asking, "New York?" and Jan Koffer nodded his head.

"Hudson River? " was followed by another nod.

"Erie Canal!" In response, Jan proudly replied in English. "Low bridge, everybody down."

Two hours later, they came to another lock, which seemingly was leading them right into the mountain ridge! The boat captain pointed his hand up to confirm that they would travel to the top. The Hollanders were still not used to the mountains and even less so to the concept that a boat could travel up a mountainside! In Holland, the only peaks they had seen, were the three or four-story city buildings lining the canals. The mountain peaks along the Hudson were much higher but the steamboat traveled between them and the river level did not change much. How could a boat be raised to the top of such a high mountain ridge?

Teunis Koeffers wondered if the line boat would be lifted up with ropes. He was familiar with the Dutch method of moving furniture to the top city apartments. Because the staircases were steep and narrow, each tall Dutch building had overhanging beams. Large furniture pieces would be lifted with ropes and then pulled through the windows.

Higher and higher the boat traveled through the canal locks and yet at each level there were more towering heights above them. Looking east, one could see the Hudson valley, with more mountain ranges on the horizon. They spent most of their first day passing through nearly twenty locks and ended up more than one hundred sixty feet higher. At this point they were close to Cohoes Falls where the Mohawk River cascaded down to the Hudson River Valley. Actually most of the river water had been diverted in 1825 to operate the new Erie Canal locks. The portion of the Mohawk River water, which was allowed to flow freely over the falls, would take just one hour to reach the Hudson River.

The boats continued through more locks. Finally, they reached the first section of the canal cut through a relatively flat section of the land, just above the Mohawk River valley. A new teamster took over the horses. He was an even younger boy, perhaps fifteen, and was short and scruffy. He spent his time chewing tobacco, glancing a few times back at the immigrants on the deck of the boat. After a while he started to sing, alternating between poignant and cheery songs. In the middle of the fifth song, he abruptly stopped and resumed chewing tobacco.

As they traveled further, the walls of the canal became higher. It was getting dark and only occasional dim treetops could be seen from the boat. The passengers still on deck returned to the cabin to take up their sleeping quarters. Some of the elders, who had spent the previous night in the canvas bunks, decided to sleep on the floor. Once again all available space was occupied, with the Hollanders spread, one next to another, on the floor and on the tables.

Soon the cabin became stuffy and a window was partly opened. Sometime later they woke up to the swooshing sound of water and the rocking of the boat. A girl screamed, "We are sinking."

More shrieks followed before some man offered an explanation. The rocking of the boat and the sound of the water was the same as when they had been passing through the locks. It was just a different sensation when one was sound asleep and laying in darkness at the bottom of the cabin. Shortly after passing through that lock, the line boat stopped for the night.

Early next morning, the boat resumed the journey. Many Hollanders stepped out on the deck to catch some fresh air. It was freezing outside and the passengers alternated between staying on deck and returning to the stuffy cabin. The high walls of the canal mostly blocked the view of the land around them. Only in the distance could they see the tops of distant peaks and mountain ranges.

Later in the morning, the Hollanders observed an amazing event. The canal was changing course to cross over the Mohawk River, which was flowing directly below them! The passengers crowded on top of the barge to observe the perplexing canal-over-river intersection. The boat was traveling over an aqueduct bridge, with the water constrained by stonewalls. Below them the river was flowing in a deep gorge cut by its fierce current.

Soon the canal changed course again and began to follow the river along the other shore. The aqueduct was a very elaborate and expensive structure. It was hard to understand why the canal route was switched from one side of the river to another. Blish decided to ask the captain about it.

The captain replied that the route had been picked by the civil engineers to minimize the overall construction cost. They would pass through more than a dozen of aqueducts before reaching Buffalo. The aqueducts were expensive but when one side of the river became uneven it was best to switch to the other side. Sometimes the canal route departed miles away from the rivers it generally followed.

The captain added. "You know that the Erie Canal is considered one of the great wonders of the world. Many civil engineers from Europe came here to study the locks and the methods used by the canal designers to prevail over the mountains. The canal became an immediate financial success and was already expanded once. The Erie Canal has been instrumental in opening up Western New York, Pennsylvania, Ohio, and the New Territories around Lake Michigan. Most settlers have used the canal on the way to their destinations. The Erie Canal still provides the only economical way to ship the settlers' grain and other goods to the East Coast."

Chapter 11

Schenectady – Erie Canal

Schenectady, "Marco Paul's Travels on the Erie Canal"
by HLP Publishing

By mid afternoon on Saturday, October 30th, the line boat had reached Schenectady. The town had a population of eight thousand and became prosperous as the transfer center between the railroad and the Erie Canal. Its name was of Indian origin and meant the "end of the pine plains." The early history was full of horror for the original Dutch settlers. In 1690, Indians and French soldiers from Canada raided and massacred most of the inhabitants. The Dutch influence was still strong in 1820 when a section of Schenectady was detached to form a township of Rotterdam.

The Erie Canal was extra wide while passing through town, with steep stone-lined banks. A row of three-story-tall buildings and shops ran parallel to the canal. Next to one of the bridges was a narrow dock with steps leading to the top. An empty packet boat was tied up there, ready for the passengers departing in the evening. The packet boat was the same size as the line boat except that the cabin ran almost the full length of the boat.

Somewhere close by a loud steam whistle was heard. Jan Koeffers turned to his friend David Blish and asked "steamship?" Blish shook his head, explaining in English that it was a train. Noticing that Jan did not understand him, Blish repeated slowly, "No steamships on the canal; steam locomotive from Albany to Schenectady and then to Buffalo." Blish was surprised that Jan still did not catch on so he drew a picture of a train with the smoke rising from the locomotive.

Jan finally understood the explanation and smiled. He never saw a train in his whole life but was familiar with the train pictures in books and newspapers. Trains were common in Germany and England but in the whole of Holland there were only six miles of railroad tracks. This was due to the geography of Holland where much of the land was below the sea level. To reach the sea, rivers flowed in steep embankments, raised above the countryside, which obstructed the train tracks. The children were excited that soon they would be able to finally see a moving train.

The line boat continued to travel through the town. Groups of onlookers lined the canal banks, waving to the passengers standing on the deck of the passing boat. At one point, several musicians played on a bridge, spanning the two sides of the town. Jan Koeffers exclaimed, "The people welcome us with music because we come from Europe?"

Blish smiled. "Crossing the Atlantic is a big achievement but they are not playing music to salute you. There are many boats with European immigrants passing here every day. It is Saturday afternoon and the town people are probably celebrating some special occasion. Enjoy the music and the scenery of a prosperous town."

The boat stopped briefly and the tired horses were changed for fresh ones. The passengers used the occasion to get out and stretch their legs. Soon the helmsman waived to them to return to the boat but a few young Hollanders motioned that they wanted to walk along with the horses on the towpath. After spending two months on the ocean, it was nice to get some exercise.

The young men had no trouble keeping up with the horses. In fact, soon they started showing off, walking quickly and passing the horses behind them. At first, the elders frowned at those young men. After a while they decided, however, that, at the next stopover, they also would walk on the towpath. It would be a good exercise and they could have a better view of the countryside.

The land close to the canal was a mixture of pastures and fields already harvested and left fallow for the winter. Occasionally they passed orchards and groves of trees. Only a few homes were visible, larger and better kept than the cottages in Holland. The homes were scattered far apart unlike the dwellings in the old country, which were normally grouped together in villages.

A shrill steam whistle was heard in the distance, a precursor of the excitement of the day. Soon a locomotive was in full view and Jan Koeffers alerted the passengers inside of the cabin, "A train is about to pass us, right by the canal!"

The teamster immediately grabbed the tow horses to keep them from panicking. The train rushed right past the line boat, a few passengers waving from the train windows. It was an amazing sight: train cars moving faster than a galloping horse. Jan was most impressed, "If we had taken the train, we could be in Buffalo tomorrow."

His father Teunis Koeffers watched the train with fear, recalling minister Wyckoff's warnings about the numerous accidents. "It is best not to use the devil's contraptions or one will end up indebted to the evil one. That's why some in our group swore never to travel by train. In any case, the trains charge extra for baggage and I would rather save my money to buy more land."

Jan protested that their neighbors in Germany commonly used trains. Furthermore the trains used the same steam engines as the steamship they had traveled on the Hudson River.

Teunis Koeffers sternly lectured his son. "Innovations are acceptable as long as they are used prudently. A steamship would never outrace a galloping horse. As for the Germans, if they continue to travel by trains, they will become indebted to the devil and lose their souls."

The boat traveled for hours, occasionally passing through more locks. The Hollanders paid little notice to the names of the communities they were passing by. Their attention definitely perked up when Blish told Jan that the next large village would be Amsterdam. Animated, they asked Jan to translate their questions, "Why is this community named after the second largest Dutch city and are there many Hollanders living there?"

Blish turned to the boat captain for the additional information on Amsterdam. It was a large prosperous village with a population around two thousand people, originally named Veddersburg. Some forty years earlier, the inhabitants had voted to change the name to Amsterdam to honor the early Dutch settlers. The captain did not know anybody in Amsterdam who could still speak Dutch but there were still many people of Dutch ancestry. A number of industrial mills operated in Amsterdam because of the ample waterpower from the

Chuctanunda Creek.

Soon the cook started to serve supper. The Hollanders still considered the generous portions of fried pork chops and fresh bread a splendid meal. Afterwards a small boy asked if there would be oranges or apples for dessert. His father lectured him, "Don't be greedy and never ask for something which is not offered."

Sometime after supper, the Erie Canal again crossed the Mohawk River on an aqueduct. Most of the passengers came up on the deck to view the river flowing in a gorge below the canal. The first time the canal had passed over the river, the view generated amazement. This time the sight was still interesting but the passengers were baffled why the canal builders kept switching the route from one side of the river to the other. It would take a civil engineer, however, to explain how the terrain determined the optimum canal course.

After an overnight stopover, the line boat continued early in the morning on its journey. They passed through another large village, Canajoharie. It had a population of over four thousand and was known for mills powered by ample water from the Canajoharie Creek. Its old Iroquois Indian name meant "the pot that washes itself" and was based on the nearby gorge section carved by the fiercely flowing water.

The boat passed through more locks and the countryside grew more hilly and wild. At one point the passengers spotted a small herd of deer drinking water from the canal. The deer raised their heads, startled by the horses towing the barge on the opposite side of the canal.

As the deer scattered, a dark shape broke from the nearby bushes. The passengers watched a lone wolf attack an unlucky fawn which was knocked down to the ground. Hearing the cry of the fawn, its mother turned back. Sprinting directly toward the wolf, the doe kicked it viciously with its front legs. The startled wolf jumped back then started to snarl and advance forward again. The doe bravely stood her ground, timing another vicious kick just as the wolf lounged forward. The wolf yelped then started to snarl at the doe again. Slowly the fawn got back on her legs and stood there, injured and dazed by the developments. The standoff continued, even as the barge slowly passed by.

Jan Koffer paid a moving tribute to the drama with his favorite phrase learned during the transatlantic passage. Turning toward Blish, he said, "America, home of the brave."

Late in the afternoon the line boat reached the Little Falls. They passed through a series of additional locks, climbing ever higher into the small mountain ranges. It rained most of the time and the passengers stayed in the cabins. At night it was damp, cold, and seemingly even more crowded as the passengers stretched out wherever they could.

The weather cleared up during the night. The line boat started to travel again just before dawn and a number of Hollanders came up on deck. That day they would travel through several larger villages and towns on the canal named after the ancient old world cities. The first one was Ilion, which was a Greek name for Troy. Ilion was best known for the rifles made by the Remington family.

The boat captain proudly showed Blish his own rifle he had bought from Mr. Remington. Eliphalet Remington had made his first gun thirty years earlier when he was in his early twenties. Guns were very expensive so he searched his father's forge shop for scrap iron chunks. He then heated and forged the thin slab around a rod whose diameter was equal to the rifle's bore. Afterwards, he lap-welded the edges, pulled out the rod, and had a nearby gunsmith complete the bore rifling. The neighbors and acquaintances were impressed with the rifle and asked him to make some for them. Soon he had so many orders for the guns that he had to move to a larger shop.

Blish inspected the captain's splendid rifle but could find no sign of welding. "I will bet that in our days all rifles are made by boring a hole in a solid rod."

The captain grinned. "You would lose your bet. Many gunsmiths have experimented with machines for boring the rifle hole out of bars. Nonetheless, all production rifles are still made today the same way as that first one made by Mr. Remington in his youth. You can't see the weld on this barrel because it has been ground off and then polished."

Sometime later the line boat passed through a much larger city of Utica with a population of seventeen thousand. Utica was named after the North African city, which had become the capital of the Roman province in Africa after the destruction of Carthage. By the end of the day, the line boat reached the city of Rome itself, slightly smaller than Utica. The fourteen-mile canal section between the two cities had been built between 1817 and 1819 as the first phase of the Erie Canal. Both cities became very prosperous, with numerous work yards and terminals along the canal. There were few streams in the area to provide the waterpower for the mills but the new industries thrived on steam power.

At Rome, the Erie Canal reached its peak elevation of 420 feet above sea level. It was the end of the route along the Mohawk River, which had cut a passage between the Catskills and the Adirondack Mountains. They had covered 125 miles and had fewer than 240 miles left to reach Buffalo.

The following day the line boat traveled fourteen miles through more locks and descended to an elevation fifty feet lower. Further on, they passed close to Lake Oneida, one of the few New York "finger" lakes running east to west. Later the canal followed for sixteen miles along the Oneida River, which twisted through countryside like a slithering snake. After that, the canal followed the Seneca River.

Eventually the boat reached Syracuse, a canal boomtown with a population of 20,000. It was known as the "salt city" and dozens of barges were being loaded with that and other commodities. A few hours after passing through Syracuse, the line boat entered the aqueduct over the Montezuma Swamp. During the canal construction, over one thousand workers died of malaria in this section. Many men died within days of being hired. Soon the local farmers refused to work there and the jobs were filled mainly by the desparate Irish emigrants.

The work in the swamp was only completed during the winter when the mosquitoes were no longer biting the workers. The construction of the canal resulted in draining most of the marshes and the rich muckland became highly valued agricultural land.

The next day, the boat traveled over the relatively flat countryside with only a few locks to lift it higher again. The weather was cloudy but dry and many passengers chose to walk on the towpath. Walking helped to pass the time and it was preferable to the idleness in the cabin or on the crowded top deck.

The following day the terrain became steeper and they navigated through a series of locks. They passed many small communities along the canal, some well known for quite exclusive products. Lyons was an international exporter of peppermint while Newark was famous for roses and perfume oils.

Another much smaller community was known as the birthplace of the Mormon Church in 1830. The boat captain remembered the Mormon leader, Joseph Smith, and was glad that he moved with his followers first to Ohio, and then to Missouri and Illinois. People were wary of the new religion and there were conflicts and violence wherever the Mormons attempted to settle down.

Days passed as the line boat continued its travel on the

canal. The new sights and communities no longer attracted much attention. The Dutch immigrants were curious only about the land prices. They were surprised to learn that it would be difficult to find any land near the canal for less than one hundred dollars an acre. It was best to hurry up to the New Territories where the land was still cheap.

The immigrants assumed that the further they traveled on the Erie Canal, the fewer people they would encounter in the settlements. That premise was proven false once again when the line boat approached Rochester. They learned from the captain that Rochester's population was thirty five thousand people, almost as large as the state capital Albany on the Hudson River.

The boat captain described the incredible expansion. "Only seven hundred people lived in Rochester in 1817. All of the growth was due to the Erie Canal and the inexpensive water transportation. The nearby waterfalls provide cheap power for dozens of flourmills which ship more than half a million barrels of flour to New York."

After days spent among fields and woods, it was strange for the line boat to pass right through the center of a big city. The Genesee River divided Rochester and the canal crossed from one side to another over an eight-hundred-foot long aqueduct. Tall buildings lined the sides of the canal and the banks were full of well-dressed pedestrians.

Blish used the brief stopover to send a telegram to the Buffalo port authorities. He stated that he and a large group of Dutch immigrants would be arriving Wednesday and continuing on to Wisconsin. He received a reply that the steam-powered "propeller" *Phoenix* would be waiting for them. After passing through four more locks, the line boat entered another very long stretch of mostly flat countryside. They spent two more days there, passing through many small communities.

Finally, the line boat approached Lockport located amid

the towering hills. The city was another canal boomtown with the population close to ten thousand. The ample waterpower was the source for numerous flourmills, sawmills, and other industrial concerns. A series of five locks was necessary to lift the boats to the top of the upland. The elevation was over five hundred sixty feet higher than at their start in Albany.

They were now only thirty-one miles from Buffalo, with only one more lock to pass through. The passengers were going to spend their final night on the boat before arriving in Buffalo in the afternoon of the following day. The boat captain insisted on having the last supper with David Blish and they used the occasion to talk about their future plans.

The captain mentioned that Niagara Falls was only twenty miles away from Buffalo and wondered if Blish was planning to visit there. Many New Yorkers and even Europeans had traveled by packet boats or by trains just to visit the famous waterfall.

Blish replied, "On this trip, I have to look after my merchandise. Besides, I would not enjoy sightseeing on my own. I am planning to see Niagara Falls next time I will travel to the East Coast with my wife and our children."

The captain was also curious about the future plans of the Hollanders. He knew that Blish had become good friends with them. It was fascinating to watch this American merchant communicate with the Dutch travelers through a mixture of simple words and hand gestures.

David Blish replied that he had a high regard for his Dutch friends. "Most of them are planning to settle in Wisconsin. They appear to be relatively prosperous and left Holland due to the religious persecution. The majority of this group are experienced farmers and I am sure that they will make a fine addition to our territory."

Chapter 12

Buffalo, NY – Phoenix

Buffalo in 1825, Buffalo and Erie Country Historical Society

In 1847, Buffalo was an important port where cargoes were transferred between the Great Lakes ships and the Erie Canal boats. From spring to late fall, the harbor was always crowded, often with a hundred steamships and sailing vessels. According to the local residents, the city's name came from "beau fleuve," French for beautiful river. The population had grown from five thousand, in 1825, when the canal had opened to nearly forty thousand in 1847. Most pioneers boarded ships here on their way to the New Territories. It was also a popular destination for visitors from the East Coast who wanted to see nearby Niagara Falls.

The Buffalo waterfront was the rendezvous point for the travelers destined to sail aboard the steamship *Phoenix*. The three Erie Canal line boats carrying David Blish, the Koeffers family, and other Dutch immigrants, reached the harbor early afternoon on Wednesday, November 10th. The Hollanders carried their baggage to the *Phoenix* and then returned to carry chains and other hardware owned by Blish. Some fifty other Dutch immigrants, who had traveled by packet boats or trains, were soon located and the Dutch group was again reunited.

Their new ship was smaller and more slender than the "side-wheeler" steamship they had traveled on the Hudson River. Built in 1845, the *Phoenix* was among the few dozen of the most modern "propeller" steamships traversing the Great Lakes. The "propellers" were hardier than the steamships with side-wheels, which could be damaged in storms or by logs floating at the surface. The American patent for ship screw propulsion had been issued only in 1838 and three years later the first propeller was put in service on the Great Lakes.

Like all ships of its day, the *Phoenix's* hull was built of wood. Being primarily a cargo ship, most of the available space was used for carrying freight and "steerage" passengers. The top level consisted of accommodations for over 30 cabin passengers, plus the dining room, and quarters for the officers and the crew. Above the top deck were the pilothouse and three lifeboats, one on each side and at the stern. A single mast and a twenty-foot long rolled-iron funnel completed the topside silhouette. The *Phoenix*, 143 feet long and 26 feet wide, had capacity to carry 300 tons of cargo and passengers.

On the westward voyages, the *Phoenix's* cargo holds were often filled with over 200 immigrant steerage passengers plus hardware, coffee, sugar, and other goods from the East Coast. On the return voyage, the cargo consisted mostly of wheat, fish barrels, and other food products.

Captain Benjamin Sweet, the *Phoenix*'s master and the ship's part owner, was pleased to see so many immigrants coming aboard. It was the end of the shipping season and he was concerned that the ship would leave half-empty.

Captain Sweet was one of the most experienced steamship captains on the Great Lakes. He was well liked by his crew, as he was not a strict disciplinarian. His philosophy was to select the best men available and to train and motivate them well.

Like all other skippers, Captain Sweet was not averse to taking calculated risks. Sometimes it was a choice between proceeding in a storm and running for the safety of some harbor. Other times, it was a matter of helping people and trusting that they would repay their debt.

The highlight of Captain Sweet's career was the occasion when he saved nearly the entire population of Duluth, Minnesota from likely starvation. The new settlers there found the hard way that crops would fail in the area's mineral-rich soil. With winter approaching, the inhabitants had little food and no money to buy tickets to more prosperous communities. Captain Sweet allowed seven hundred passengers to travel on his ship by accepting their "I owe you" signed notes. The greatly overloaded ship sailed on until it could drop off the passengers in communities where work and shelter were available for the winter. All but one of those promissory notes were eventually paid off.

Captain Sweet prospered by taking calculated risks but the latest one tarnished his reputation. Just days earlier, his ship crossed paths with a side-wheeler steamer a few miles from Cleveland. The *Phoenix* had the right of way but Captain Sweet knew that Great Lakes skippers loved to challenge each other. Often the two ships plowed straight ahead until the meeker captain would turn aside. Captain Sweet maintained his course, somewhat altering it at the last moment. He expected the other captain to also alter his course but his assumption was wrong.

The two ships collided. Fortunately, the *Phoenix* received just a slight blow and emerged with only minor bow damage. At Buffalo, most of the broken sections were repaired and the bow was repainted. Full repairs would be performed after their return to Cleveland for the winter. In the meantime, the ship was perfectly safe to sail. Still, some superstitious sailors felt that only a complete repair would remove the bad omen.

The old mariners evoked superstition to explain the hundreds of ships and boats scattered at the bottom of the Great Lakes. The westbound ships first crossed Lake Erie and then had to travel north on Lake Huron and south on Lake Michigan. The sailors noted that the last two lakes resembled a giant horseshoe. The trouble was that the "horseshoe" appeared on the map upside down, with the prongs pointing down. That position insured that all the luck would fall out.

With or without superstition, a collision was a black mark on the captain's record. It was also a nuisance to deal with the authorities and the insurance investigators. Captain Sweet was glad that it was almost the end of the shipping season. Only one more run remained from Buffalo to Wisconsin and Chicago and then back to homeport in Cleveland. The weather was already foul but at least the ship would be carrying a lot of passengers and the cruise would be very profitable.

The Dutch immigrant group, who had to split up in Albany to travel in separate boats, became once again reunited aboard the *Phoenix*. The total number of Hollanders had actually increased. The Albany group was joined by additional Dutch families, which had crossed the Atlantic on different ships.

Thirty-four of the Dutch newcomers were from Wisch/Varsseveld. They consisted of six families: Colenbrander, Oberink, Te Kotte, Wildenbeest. Gielink, Nebbelink, and Toebes.

Fourteen people were from Aalten: the Navis family of eight, the Kraayenbrink family of five plus the young farmer Jan Brusse. The other newcomers were the Bruijel family of six and Gerrit Demkes and his mother.

Several dozens of steerage passengers from other countries clustered in their own groups and appeared to be baffled by the dominant Dutch conversations. Three German families were the first to board the ship and had settled in the bunks closest to the ladder. An Irish farm family of eight formed their own group, together with six young Irish itinerant laborers.

One odd steerage passenger was a thirty-year-old Norwegian lumberjack. He appeared frustrated by his inability to communicate with the other passengers. He had lived in America for several years and kept on repeating the words "Norwegian— lumberjack" to the various groups. He was finally "adopted" by the Irish family.

The matronly wife of the Irish immigrant turned to the lumberjack to complain about the overcrowded steerage compartment. "There must be over two hundred steerage passengers here and more will show up before the departure in the morning. It's my husband's fault that we are packed here like fish in a barrel. We could have left yesterday on another steamship, which departed half empty. But no, my husband wanted to wait an extra day so we could join up with some Irish compatriots."

The man merely replied, "I cut trees in America, Norwegian—lumberjack." The Irish family quickly found out that the lumberjack's English was limited to only a few dozen words, most of them concerning food and drinks.

Late Wednesday evening, the first mate knocked on the captain's door. Inside, Mr. Watts reported on preparations for the next day's departure. Most of the information was routine. At one point, Mr. Watts summarized his conversation with two passengers planning to travel to Fairport, Ohio. It was a small village twenty-five miles from Cleveland, which was always bypassed by the large all-passenger steamships. The *Phoenix* had a less rigid schedule and could stop at any small port, providing the weather permitted it. The Fairport passengers were expected to board the ship in the morning, just before the departure.

"I warned those men that if the weather remained foul, they would have to get off in Cleveland and travel to Fairport from there. They replied that they would each pay an extra dollar to insure that the ship does stop in Fairport...."

Captain Sweet's eyes sparkled at the mention of the extra money. It was a common practice to keep some of the income unreported to the other ship's owners. The only accurate records were those on the number of the cabin passengers and on the insured cargo. In contrast, the number of the immigrant steerage passengers was often underreported, with the proceeds kept by the captain.

There was no danger that the first mate would ever question the captain's right to keep part of the revenues. Mr. Watts was an experienced mariner, eager to assume his own command, and quite aware that he depended on Captain Sweet to recommend him for a promotion. The captain and the first mate both lived in Cleveland and knew each other's professional and social lives. On the whole, they were both good officers and they commanded a fine ship.

The captain sensed that the first mate was concerned about stopping in Fairport due to foul weather and the possibility of damage to the ship during docking. The first mate still had to get used to the concept of calculated risks.

"Mr. Watts, in the past we have made many stops under similar conditions and with no two-dollar premium offered. I know that Lake Erie has the worst gales out of all the Great Lakes. The weather fronts all seem to collide here and churn up the shallow waters. But we also must be willing to accommodate our passengers. Let's delay for now the final decision on whether we will stop in Fairport until we see what's the weather tomorrow."

The captain and his mate next proceeded to review the status of the crew. The captain was pleased to hear that the crewmen from Cleveland were all aboard: Mr. House, Chief Engineer, D. W. Keller, steward, T. S. Donahue, clerk, E. Watts, second porter, and John Mann, deckhand. Also aboard were John Nugent, first fireman from Buffalo, J.C. Smith, saloonkeeper, Horace Tisdale, cabin boy, four deckhands, and the two colored cooks.

Still ashore were Newell Merrill, second mate from Ohio City, William Owen, second engineer from Toledo, Luther Southward, wheelsman from New Bedford, Hugh Robinson, first porter from Chicago, Michael O'Brien, fireman from Buffalo, and the two Canadian deckhands.

Hearing the report, the captain winced, annoyed that two of his officers still ashore were probably drinking. "Mr. Watts, aren't you concerned about Mr. Merrill and Mr. Owen? I am not surprised at the deckhands spending their free time in taverns but I would expect this ship's officers to be more restrained. I think you should have a talk with Mr. Merrill and Mr. Owen about their drinking habits."

The first mate knew that the captain's directive was justified. The two officers did spend more money on spirits than what would be considered appropriate. Furthermore, one of them was married with small children and probably not providing well for his family. On the other hand, it had been a long shipping season and the two men were friends and in need of some distraction.

Mr. Watts confirmed that the captain's orders would be carried out. "I will talk to the two men and warn them not to do it again. It is important for the officers to maintain the appearance of respectability. At the same time, I am certain that all officers and crewmen will be quite able to perform their duties when the ship sails in the morning."

The captain knew that all men were anxious to complete the final cruise and get home for the holidays. The officers were all likely to be back next spring as soon as the ice would melt on the rivers connecting the Great Lakes. Some of the deckhands would never be seen again, lured by better pay or perhaps by a tale of better meals. Food was very important to the mariners who spent three quarters of the year eating aboard the ship.

The original ship's cook got married one year ago and got pressured by his wife to stay home and run an inn. His colored assistant took over temporarily until they could find a permanent cook. The crew liked his food, however, and eventually the captain decided to keep him and hire his cousin as a helper.

At first, the company officials put pressure on the captain to reverse his decision. "The passengers will complain about the food and refuse to travel again on a ship with a black cook. You will have trouble hiring new crewmen who will sign up on ships with better cooks."

In response, Captain Sweet invited the officials to dine aboard his ship. The dishes were delicious, just like those prepared by the ship's original cook. The cabin passengers compared it very favorably with meals served in restaurants. The ship's crew started to spread tales in taverns about their cook who took time to prepare anything they fancied.

Those images from the past flashed through captain's mind then vanished as he refocused on the business on hand. After the update about the crew, he listened to the first mate's report on the status of the cargo and passengers. In the cabin section, twenty-one passengers were already embarked. More passengers were likely to arrive in the morning, just before departure.

The steerage section, on the other hand, was already full with over two hundred mostly Dutch passengers.

The ship, in fact, was already overloaded as it also carried a heavy load of hardware, coffee, sugar, molasses, and other products. The cargo was insured for twelve thousand dollars. The majority of the steerage passengers and cargo were heading to Wisconsin, which meant full fares and a very profitable journey.

The first mate went over the list of the cabin passengers, many of them also heading for Wisconsin. Traveling to Southport was Mr. Blish plus Mr. Fink with his wife. Mr. West, his wife, and child were going to Racine while Mr. Long, his wife, and child, were getting off in Milwaukee. Several more families were traveling to Ohio and Illinois destinations.

After completing the report, Mr. Watts paused, and then asked a question that was bothering him. "The *Phoenix* is starting out with only half a load of wood used as fuel for the boilers. With foul weather and the heavy cargo, there will be little spare fuel for any delays or emergencies."

The captain knew that the heavy load and bad weather would increase the fuel consumption. "I am confident that we have enough fuel to get to Detroit where wood is less expensive. We will keep our eye on the fuel consumption and, if needed, we will get additional supplies during the stopover in Cleveland."

Captain Sweet paused and then revealed a different concern that had been bothering him. "The old sailing ships would finish the season at the beginning of November because of the foul weather. With steamships, we have been stretching the shipping season, sometimes perhaps too much." The captain sighed then concluded, "Well, at least we have the finest propeller on the Great Lakes and don't need to worry about the wind ripping our sails and capsizing us."

Chapter 13

Lake Erie

Phoenix, Historical Collections of the Great Lakes, Bowling Green SU

The calendar in the captain's cabin showed the following data for Thursday, November 11th: sunrise at 6:45 AM and sunset at 5:37 PM. It was still dark when Captain Sweet, the master of the *Phoenix*, had his breakfast. Afterwards, he climbed to the top deck to oversee the final preparations for the departure. Nine additional passengers, most of them men, bought tickets in the morning to Cleveland and other destinations. Usually there would be more families traveling to nearby ports but the weather remained stormy and those who had a choice would postpone their trips.

At 7:30 AM, a coach arrived at the landing and a middle-aged man emerged, unfolding an umbrella for protection from the pouring rain. As he approached the ship, the man asked to talk to the captain.

Captain Sweet was near the gangway and asked the man how he could help him.

"We wish to buy tickets for our two nieces to return them to their parents in Sheboygan, Wisconsin." Glancing at the dark clouds, the man continued, "We are concerned, however, about the stormy weather and the shipboard accommodations for the two girls."

The captain asked whether anybody would be accompanying the nieces.

"No, they will be traveling alone. My wife's nieces had come to Cleveland to live in a boarding school. They got homesick and came to us for help to get the ship tickets. We want them to spend Christmas with their parents, providing it is safe to do so."

Captain Sweet assured the man that the girls would be perfectly safe aboard the *Phoenix*. "The weather is foul but for the steamship passengers, heavy seas entail only a bit of discomfort. Detroit is only two days away. After that, we will be traveling on Lake Huron and Lake Michigan, which generally are less stormy. The girls will be fine with us and, most likely, it is their last chance to get home for the holidays."

The man went back to the coach and returned with his wife, her nieces, and their trunks. The husband introduced Elisa Hazelton, the pretty fourteen-year old with long brunette pigtails, and then Anna, the eleven-year old with short blonde locks. The girls appeared happy and relieved that they would be allowed to proceed on their journey to rejoin the parents.

Captain Sweet smiled as he greeted the girls. "Welcome aboard. The boys in Buffalo will be sorry to see you two beauties return to the New Territories. It will be Buffalo's loss and Sheboygan's gain when you get back there."

Horace Tisdale, the cabin boy, took the girls' luggage and led them to their cabin. He was only a year older than Eliza and completely embarrassed to be alone with the two young girls. Eliza explained that they were going home to spend Christmas with their parents. She asked the cabin boy whether he would be home for the holidays with his family.

The boy shrugged, "I haven't decided yet. My father is dead and my stepfather takes all my money when I come home. I would like to see my mother and two sisters though...."

The skies remained dark gray and a strong wind whipped the riggings on the ship. At least the rain had lessened and the visibility improved somewhat. At 8:05 AM, Captain Sweet issued orders to cast off the lines.

The waves outside the harbor were four to five feet high, capped with white foam. The passengers had a hard time getting used to walking on deck which rocked below their feet. The lake waves were much closer to each other than ocean swells and they relentlessly pounded the ship. The *Phoenix* soon settled into a rhythmic pattern of sideways rolls and forward lurches, rising and then dropping over the top of the waves. The shores remained visible but the bad weather kept the passengers from staying on deck to observe the scenery.

Within an hour, several steerage passengers were at the ship's guardrails, struggling with their seasickness. Many other travelers in the cargo compartment felt queasy and wondered how to get to the stairs. It was dark there and difficult to walk as all open space was filled with baggage and stretched-out people. Small children took turns crying and sobbing, as their mothers attempted to comfort them.

A young boy whispered, "Father, do the sea monsters live only in the oceans or are they also in the Great Lakes?" The man replied that they saw no sea monsters in the Atlantic and they would see none in the lakes. The boy persisted. "But a sea monster cloud followed us in the Atlantic and then the crew threw Jan Essenlinkpas' body in the ocean...."

The father grew angry. "Jan Essenlinkpas died from sickness and was buried at sea. You children were all told not to mention the sea monsters again. We have survived a two-month crossing of the Atlantic on a sailing ship. Now we have only a week's journey left on the most modern propeller steamship. We need to offer thanks to our Lord for bringing us safely to our promised land."

Hours passed as the ship plowed through the waves, generally within the sight of land. Lake Erie was about sixty miles wide and two hundred forty miles long. The *Phoenix* was to make a brief stopover at Fairport and then continue to Cleveland, both on the western end of Lake Erie. Due to rough weather, lunch for the cabin passengers was limited to steak sandwiches and hot drinks. The captain joined the passengers and asked them to introduce themselves.

David Blish stated that he was from Southport, Wisconsin, along with his neighbors, Mr. and Mrs. Fink. Across the table were Edwin West, his wife, and their child, residents of Racine, just ten miles north of Southport. Next to them were Mr. J. Long, his wife, and their child who were from Milwaukee. The final two passengers at the captain's table were Eliza and Anna Hazelton who stated that they were from Sheboygan.

The captain addressed the girls. "Students at the boarding schools usually stay there for the whole school year. I am curious why you decided to go home for Christmas since no ships will sail again for Buffalo until spring?"

Eliza sighed. "The girls at the boarding school called us savages from the New Territories. They claimed that we eat raw meat and dance with bears. We are not going back there ever again." David Blish grinned and stated that the Wisconsin bears possessed more social graces than some folks from New York. Laughter followed and introductions resumed at the second table.

Hamlin Heath introduced his group of seven passengers, originally from Binghamption, New York. They were traveling to Littleport, Illinois and from there to the Bureau County where they were planning to buy farmland. Next to Heath were his wife Sarah and their child. Next to Sarah were Ramsey and Amanda Austin who were her brother and sister. The last two members of the group were Heath's brother-in-law David Austin and his child.

The next passenger at the table, J. Burrows, merely stated that he was returning to Chicago, Illinois. Clarence O'Connor was the last person to introduce himself, his wife, and their daughter. He said that they were from Ireland and were going to visit Milwaukee and Chicago.

The captain was intrigued. Not many travelers from a famine stricken country would travel in the ship's expensive cabin section and declare themselve to be visitors. It would be inappropriate to ask how they could afford such a journey. At the same time, the captain hoped that an indirect comment would prompt the Irish couple to explain their travel objectives.

"You do know that the shipping season on the Great Lakes finishes at the end of this month. If you are a visitor, you have to be prepared to remain here until the spring."

O'Connor's wife interjected with a brief explanation but without giving full details. "We heard a lot fascinating stories about the New Territories and decided to visit the new towns and settlements. We may buy land in Wisconsin but first will spend a winter in the area to find out if the climate is agreeable."

David Blish corroborated that many Irish farmers had settled in the hilly sections of Central Wisconsin, twenty to thirty miles away from Lake Michigan. Perhaps the hilly countryside reminded the Irish of their own land.

The *Phoenix* changed course and the ship's rolling became more pronounced. Edwin West asked whether the bad weather could endanger their ship. The captain assured him that the *Phoenix* could safely sail through the worst storms. In any case, the conditions were likely to improve, after they would leave Lake Erie behind.

Mrs. West queried the captain about a different hazard. "Almost every year there are newspaper accounts of steamships catching fire. How safe is our ship and why are there so many fire tragedies?"

The captain's face turned stern "There was never a deadly fire aboard a ship I have commanded. Small fires can start in the galley or the boiler room but an alert crew will put it out immediately. Throughout our journey, the *Phoenix* will generally sail within the sight of land. Even in case of a larger fire, there will always be enough steam in the boiler to reach the safety of the shore."

A moment of discomfited silence followed. Captain Sweet decided to change the subject by describing the ports they would be visiting along the way. "Our first stop will be Fairport, Ohio, 170 miles from Buffalo, which we will reach tomorrow morning. The next stopover will be Cleveland, 25 miles further west. From there, we will cross 100 miles across Lake Erie, sail up the Detroit River, and reach Detroit on Saturday. Afterwards, we will sail close to 300 miles across Lake Huron to Mackinac Straits. From there, the ship will traverse another 250 miles across Lake Michigan, before reaching Sheboygan, Wisconsin. After several more stops and 140 more miles, the *Phoenix* will finally reach Chicago. Altogether, the journey would take a week and cover just over 1000 miles."

After giving those detailed explanations, the captain quickly consumed his sandwich. It was not a good time to linger at the dining table. The plates and cups had to be restrained or else they would slide on the table. The cooks were anxious to secure the pans and dishes. Horace Tisdale, the cabin boy, scurried to pick up the cups and dishes from the table. Soon the dining room was empty.

Back in their cabin, Mrs. O'Connor sat next to her husband and put her head on his shoulder. "Thank you for buying the cabin tickets for this journey. I would not mind being in the steerage section if we were traveling with neighbors or friends. But certainly in this weather it's nice to be in a more spacious cabin and be able to see light through the porthole. I did not see you much when you worked twelve hours, six days a week, in the knitting mill. This trip is our first real vacation and I really do feel like a tourist."

The rain turned heavy in the afternoon. The steerage passengers were confined to their dark cargo hold. They ate bread and sausages bought at a waterfront store in Buffalo. The steerage section had no provisions for cooking or even boiling water. Fortunately, the ship's cook brought them a large pot of hot coffee. It was just big enough so that all adults and most children could have a cup of the hot beverage.

The rough weather and the crowded quarters were a disappointment to the Dutch travelers who had already spent over two months in dismal conditions. Gerrit Geerlings did his best to cheer up those around him.

"We can thank God that, in one more week, we will finally reach our destination. In bad weather, it is good to know that the ship is always sailing close to shore. I am also glad that we will be able to buy fresh bread when the ship makes stops along the way."

Teunis Koffers nodded his head in agreement and then questioned Geerlings. "Your family would be a lot more comfortable if you would move to the cabin section. I know from Mr. Blish that there are some empty cabins and the extra cost should not make that much difference to you."

Geerlings just smiled while his wife replied. "We crossed the Atlantic in the steerage quarters with our neighbors and we will complete our journey among our countrymen. There is only one week left and we must all support each other. This first night will be difficult but we can get used to anything."

Friday morning the gale diminished somewhat. Outside, the drizzle droplets were hard to distinguish from the spray whipped by the wind from the white-capped waves. The hatches to the steerage compartment were partially opened to alleviate the stuffy air. A few passengers came up on the deck to catch some fresh air and to observe the scenery along the distant shore.

Throughout the morning, the weather remained stormy but, at this point, the ship was heading straight into the wind and the rolling decreased somewhat. The *Phoenix* plowed steadily through the waves, always within sight of land. In the dining room, breakfast was served. The steerage passengers ate the bread and sausages they had brought with them. The ship's cook brought them another pot of hot coffee, which was eagerly shared. The steerage compartment was stuffy and crowded. At least the space was fairly warm, especially the sections located close to the boiler and the funnel.

Soon after breakfast, the wind changed direction and grew stronger again. The ship rolled and lurched as it sliced through some waves and was lifted up by the others. Fairport, their destination, was still not visible. Captain Sweet asked Mr. House, the chief engineer, if it possible to get more power?

The chief engineer replied, "The engine room has been running at maximum power all along. In fact, I am a bit concerned about the fast rate we are using up fuel due to the overloading and the heavy seas. Occasionally the propellers are spinning. partially out of the water.

The captain asked him if they would have enough fuel to get to Detroit. The engineer replied that they could get there but there was not much spare fuel for any emergencies.

The captain shrugged, "I don't expect any emergencies between here and Detroit. Besides, the final segment will be on the river where the waters will be calmer."

An hour later, the *Phoenix* reached Fairport. The stopover there was brief but a welcome respite from the rigors of the stormy waters. The population of Fairport was only five hundred people. In spite of bad weather, a dozen people came to the pier to observe the docking of a large steamship and to see the rare visitors.

The waves made it difficult to dock the ship. A crewman barely managed to fasten a line to secure the *Phoenix*. The waves then pushed the ship hard against the pier. The two passengers quickly jumped ashore and the ship immediately departed.

Captain Sweet winced hearing the sound of the ship bumping the pier. The fares from the two Fairport cabin passengers totaled five dollars plus the two-dollar premium. In stormy weather, the stopover was really a nuisance. A rolled up fishing net was used as a fender to protect the side of the ship but there was likely to be scraped paint. Along with the second mate, the captain stepped outside to inspect the likely damage.

Leaning over the lifeline, the captain saw a wide scratch mark in the paint but no dents. He was just turning back toward the pilothouse when the ship took an unexpected roll. Falling down, he hit his left knee hard on the cleat used for securing lines. Despite the sting of pain, the captain's first emotion was embarrassment for being caught off guard.

Mr. Merrill immediately bent down to help. Captain Sweet tried to get up but his struggles resulted in excruciating pain. The captain instructed the second mate to get help so that he could be lifted from both sides. Soon the first mate appeared along with two crewmen. Mr. Watts wanted to place the captain on a stretcher board but the captain replied that he just wanted to be lifted up.

And so it was done. The captain did not utter a single cry during that process, even though his face was twisted with pain. Supported on each side by Mr. Watts and a crewman, they reached the captain's cabin. With the captain on the mattress, Mr. Watts inspected his leg. There was a large dark swelling above the knee. The ship would reach Cleveland in about four hours and then a doctor could be called in for an examination.

Captain Sweet never cared much for the doctors. "By the time we get to Cleveland, I will be walking around on my own. Right now let's share the best medicine there is. Grab two glasses and a bottle of whiskey from my cabinet."

The firemen kept the engine at the maximum speed and the ship continued to plow through the heavy seas. The first mate stopped in the captain's cabin several times to see how he was doing. The captain refused to uncover his knee again for an inspection but it was obvious that he was in pain. He remained reluctant to call a doctor to examine his knee.

"All doctors are butchers; all they want to do is to chop off any injured limb."

The first mate simply stated they would not leave Cleveland unless a doctor first examined the captain. The captain was too much in pain to persist in his obstinacy.

The *Phoenix* arrived in Cleveland just past 7 PM. The lights of thousands of homes flickered in every direction, as appropriate for a city with a population of nearly fifteen thousand. Located at the outlet of the Ohio canal, the city was the transfer point for hundreds of thousands of barrels of flour and bushels of wheat. Cleveland's greatest attraction was a great snug harbor providing a temporary refuge from the stormy lake.

The steam whistle was sounded to let prospective passengers know that the ship was in port. As soon as the gangplank was in place, a crewman was sent for a doctor.

Forty minutes later, a coach arrived at the landing. The crewman stepped out of the door, along with a short pudgy man carrying a small handbag. The doctor was immediately taken to Captain Sweet where he proceeded to examine the swollen knee. The bones seemed to be properly aligned and there was no mention of the feared amputation. A long rest under observation was recommended. The prognosis was that the captain would regain the ability to flex his knee but it could be weeks before he could walk.

The doctor concluded with a recommendation, "For you, the shipping season is over. You need to make arrangements to be transported to your home where I will visit you every day."

The captain thanked the doctor but remained determined not to leave the ship. The transfer to his home would be painful and possibly further hurt his knee.

The doctor argued that the knee had to remain under observation but the captain merely shrugged. "If needed, I can call upon a doctor in Wisconsin or Chicago. In the meantime, I can still keep an eye on the ship's operations, even when I am confined in my cabin."

The doctor took out some medicines and instructed the first mate how to apply them. His final advice was to have a doctor inspect the captain's knee either in Milwaukee or Chicago.

An hour later, the ship was back on the open lake. The wind had picked up and shifted. The *Phoenix* was sailing on a diagonal to the rows of white-tipped waves and the rolling and the forward lurches resumed. The passengers asked Mr. Watts if they could visit the captain. The captain agreed to receive visitors but remained tense and curt.

He became more animated only when the young Hazelton sisters stopped to wish him well. The girls took time describing their life in Sheboygan and the stream of mariners and merchants passing through their father's hotel. The captain actually laughed when the younger Anna stated resolutely that both of them were planning to marry steamship captains.

"Don't marry just any steamship captain. Make sure that he is a skipper of a propeller and not a side-wheeler." The captain paused, then resumed. "Actually, only the experienced older men are likely to be chosen as captains of the propellers. Perhaps you would be better off marrying a young, clever first mate who is bound to become a propeller captain some day."

Chapter 14

Detroit - Lake Huron

Detroit in 1852, Bentley Historical Library

Just before noon on Saturday, November 13th, 1847, the *Phoenix* reached the Detroit River. For nearly 30 miles the ship traveled upriver with Michigan on the left and the Canadian province of Ontario on the right. The journey on the river was a welcome respite from the stormy lake waves and the ceaseless rolling of the ship. It was still windy and the skies remained murky but the rain had finally stopped.

Most of the steerage passengers came up on the top deck, enjoying the fresh air and the sight of the riverbanks. There were many fields with dark fertile soil but there were also a lot of unproductive stretches of woods. The Hollanders continued to be amazed that farmers' homes were so far apart.

The Dutch children started to cheer when David Blish approached and greeted them in Dutch. Those who had traveled with him on the Erie Canal line boat, had spread his reputation to all other Hollander groups. They bragged that they had learned how to speak English while he was said to be able to communicate in Dutch.

Blish repeated the two-dozen Dutch words he had previously learned. Afterwards, he changed to English with an abundant use of hand gestures. Pointing to the right side of the river, he stated that it was Canada - England. Pointing to the left, Blish explained that it was Michigan - America. He then described the fighting in this area during the Revolutionary War, using hand gestures to illustrate the roaring guns.

Blish continued with words and gestures to describe the war of 1812 during which the British again seized control of Michigan. In 1813, Commodore Perry had fought a decisive naval battle and sunk the British fleet on Lake Erie. A year later, the Americans regained full control of Detroit. Blish told the youngsters to repeat the year in English and flashed his fingers to emphasize each number. Describing the naval battle, he positioned his fingers over his forearm and exclaimed "boom, boom" to illustrate the ships firing guns. He then lowered his forearm demonstrating how the British ships sank to the bottom.

A crowd gathered as Blish continued his entertaining presentation of words and gestures. The two Hazelton sisters applauded when he finally finished by pointing to the American flag flying on the left side of the river. Blish noticed the Sheboygan girls and asked them to add something to the presentation.

The girls bowed, whispered to each, and then started to sing a popular river song.

"Oh, Shenandoah, I'm bound to leave you.
Away, you rolling river!
Oh, Shenandoah, I'll not deceive you,
Away, I'm bound away..."

While singing about the rolling river, the girls waved their hands, mimicking the earlier hand gestures made by Blish. They continued with different hand motions to interpret and emphasize each line of their song. Their performance was hilarious and Blish and the Hollanders laughed at the gentle satire.

Before long a bell was ringing to announce that supper was being served for the cabin passengers. It was the first three-course meal served since the departure from Buffalo. The ship rolling was greatly reduced on the river and the cook had a chance to show off his skills. While the turtle soup was being served, the Hazelton sisters gave an update on their earlier visit to the captain. His knee was greatly swollen and painful but he remained fairly cheerful.

The main course was a succulent lamb rib served with rice and delicious side dishes. Afterward, they were served coffee, tea, and scrumptious cakes. The steamships had a reputation for fine dining and the *Phoenix* would certainly compare favorably with the best of them.

Conversation at the table soon turned to their experiences while visiting the East Coast. Half of the passengers had lived only a few years in the New Territories but they already found life in the East too constrained. Mr. and Mrs. West visited their families partly to explore the prospect of returning there for a future retirement. Instead, they decided that their real home was in Racine and bought extra furniture and household goods to take with them.

Late in the evening, the *Phoenix* reached Detroit. It was the largest city in Michigan with a population of almost twenty thousand people. On the other side of the river was a smaller Canadian town of Windsor. Originally the French fur traders settled the area and many businesses were still run by their descendants.

The stormy night resulted in total darkness on the river. The lack of visibility meant that the *Phoenix* had to remain at the pier until daylight. In the early morning, bread and supplies were acquired for the galley.

Fresh bread was even more important for the steerage passengers who were responsible for their own food provisions. They normally ate bread with cheese or sausage three times a day, usually with hot coffee. During the Detroit stopover, the cook prepared a large pot of soup for the steerage passengers. The main ingredients were potatoes and pieces of sausage from the passengers plus vegetables and a few other contributions from the galley.

At dawn, the ship resumed travel up the Detroit River and soon entered Lake St. Clair. The weather remained stormy but the waves were only half the size of those on Lake Erie. Pressing through the white-capped waves, the ship rolled gently from side to side but the forward lurching was barely discernible. The shallow lake was nearly circular in shape. It took about four hours to cross the 22 miles distance between the mouth of the Detroit River and the outlet of the St. Clair River connecting it to Lake Huron.

Several islands marked the beginning of the St. Clair River. For 43 miles the *Phoenix* sailed upstream. Initially, the river twisted a lot before settling into a straighter quarter-mile wide channel. Rich fields and woods covered both sides of the river, with scattered settlements along the shore. Just like the Detroit River, the St. Clair River formed the border between Michigan and the Canadian province of Ontario.

The wind remained strong and intermittently pounded the

ship with heavy rain. A few times during the day the rain temporarily stopped and the passengers would crowd on the deck to catch some fresh air. David Blish usually joined his Dutch travelers, pointing out objects on the banks and saying their English names. In many ways, the scenery was similar to the Wisconsin shores along Lake Michigan.

"Land of the brave, just like Wisconsin, ja?" Blish joked to Jan Koffers.

The adults studied the shores from a more practical point of view. They noted the size of the tree trunks and estimated how much time it would take to clear an acre or to build a cabin. In Holland, most of the farmers had cut only a few trees in their entire lives and those had been smaller than what they were seeing on the shores. Buying a sharp saw would be a priority once they settled on their homesteads.

Before reaching Port Huron, the ship stopped at a settlement on the Canadian side of the river. The wood was cheaper there, sold for a dollar a cord. Loading the wood was hard work. In addition to deckhands, the steerage men were recruited to speed up the operation. The immigrants were paid for their effort with hot food and soup, which they shared with their families and friends.

It soon got dark and the shore outlines were barely visible. The *Phoenix* slowed down but continued cautiously. Just before midnight, they finally passed Port Huron and continued to Lake Huron. Large waves began to pound the ship as she plowed through the white-crested breakers. For the next 500 miles, there would be no more rivers or port calls. With foul weather, the passengers were glad that they were traveling on a reliable propeller with the land usually in sight.

Shortly after entering Lake Huron, Mr. Watts went to the captain's cabin to give an update on ship's movements. They were almost a day behind schedule. Since leaving Buffalo, the

Phoenix had averaged less than a 150 miles a day on open lakes. The sleek passenger-only propellers could steam over 200 miles a day, traveling from Buffalo to Chicago in under five days. The *Phoenix* normally took seven days but she was overloaded and was battling heavy seas. The first mate estimated that it would take them eight days to reach Chicago.

Captain Sweet was not happy. "I take great pride in my reputation for generally arriving per the announced schedule. I consider one day as the maximum tolerable delay. The weather is still bad and we must to do everything possible not to add to the delay already accumulated."

It was a long and uncomfortable night. Many immigrants stayed awake trying to visualize the conditions at their destination. They hoped for a stretch of warm dry weather to give them time to build shelter before the first snows. There was not much concern about their current journey. A seven or an eight-day passage on the Great Lakes was a trifle compared to the two-month voyage across the Atlantic in a sailing ship. Their ordeal would soon be over.

The next day the weather improved slightly and the rain diminished to an occasional drizzle. It still was windy and wet outside, with land barely visible on the horizon. The steerage passengers took turns going up on the deck to ease the overcrowding and get some fresh air. In the cabin section, the highlights of the day were the three meals served in the dining room. The passengers found the food delicious and the conversations helped to pass the time. Most travelers lingered at the table long after the food was finished.

The Hazelton sisters spent a lot of time with the captain, prodding him about his maritime adventures. At the table, they updated other passengers about the captain's condition and his colorful background. They also liked to talk about the frontier life in Sheboygan and repeated their father's tales about the mountain men in the West. The girls were often asked by other passengers to sing. They had great voices but knew the words of only a few songs and quickly grew too shy to keep repeating them.

David Blish was another popular storyteller. He talked mostly about the lives of his customers. One of the farmers frequently complained about Indians coming to his home in winter and begging for food. He generally did give them something. Afterwards, his wife berated him that his generosity meant food shortages for them in the spring. During the past winter the man was hunting deer when he was attacked and mauled by wolves. His life was saved by a group of Indians who carried him to their village and nursed him until he was able to walk again.

There were still many Indian villages along the shores of Lake Michigan. Once the land was surveyed and sold, all the Indians would be evicted to their reservations. Blish felt sorry for the Indians but also noted that many of them had moved only recently into Wisconsin after being pushed out from the East Coast. Progress could not be stopped and Indians had to learn how to farm the land, just like the European settlers.

Always curious, Blish asked O'Connor about life in Ireland and the outlook for another potato famine. He also wanted to know why the Irish people held so much resentment against the British. To help the famine victims, the Americans had sent food and money to Ireland and so did the British.

Clarence O'Connor knew that most of the passengers were of English descent and he carefully worded his response to be inoffensive. "Some British help was received in Ireland but it was too little and too late. Most land in Ireland is owned by big British landlords who have aggravated the famine crisis by evicting thousands of tenant farmers off their land. Remember that the potato famine also struck on the continent. Many people went hungry there but none starved because the continental gentry and officials were there to help their countrymen."

O'Connor paused before concluding, "We just want Ireland to be owned and governed by the Irishmen, just like you have wanted America to be governed by the Americans."

O'Connor's wife steered the conversation toward the portrayal of Ireland. She described the pastoral beauty of the Irish countryside, the fierce coastlines, and the craggy romantic highlands. Her closing statement was that, before the famine, the Irish farmers led a good life, at least those who owned their land.

Clarence O'Connor chose to end the discussion on a more assertive note. "Many outsiders have invaded Ireland over the ages. A thousand years ago, the Irish people fought the Vikings to a standstill. Likewise, we will also persevere over the British. Perhaps it is God's will to scatter millions of Irishmen to America so that we will achieve success here and eventually help bring freedom to Ireland."

Sometime later, the conversation turned to the *Phoenix's* mysterious Dutch passengers in the steerage section. Eliza Hazelton asked Blish what he knew about them and whether he had any Dutch neighbors in Southport.

Blish replied that the *Phoenix's* Dutch immigrants called themselves "Seceders" and could be best compared to the first Puritan settlers in America. "I don't know of any Dutch settlers in Southport. There is a large Dutch Seceder settlement at the western end of southern Lake Michigan. Some of the Dutch passengers are, in fact, heading for that colony. Most of them, however, are planning to join Dutch groups in Wisconsin. Many mentioned a Dutch settlement in Sheboygan County."

Elisa Hazelton confirmed that there was a small Dutch settlement in the southern part of her county. "I have seen the Dutch settlers in stores in town. They speak little English and buy tools and necessities but only at bargain prices. They are always polite and keep their clothes clean and mended."

Blish commented that the Dutch were the original settlers in New York and that many business owners and notables on the East Coast were of Dutch descent. He was certain the Dutch passengers traveling on the *Phoenix* would also do well in the Midwest.

Many more topics were raised and debated during the long hours spent in the dining room. For a day and a half, the ship plowed through the angry waves of Lake Huron. At times, the rain would diminish and the steerage passengers went topside to breath fresh air. The Dutch children patiently waited for Blish to join them and teach them more English.

Only a few passengers occasionally attempted sightseeing, normally the favorite shipboard activity. The hazy shores were too far away to study the scenery. Still, there was a growing anticipation among the Wisconsin passengers, for when they would enter Lake Michigan. Sometime Tuesday, the ship would pass through the Mackinac Straits and leave Lake Huron behind. It was their last milestone, marking the final two days before they would reach their destination.

Chapter 15

The Mackinac Straits -
Lake Michigan

Town of Mackinac, Frank Leslie's Illustrated Newspaper, 1856

The Mackinac Straits connecting Lake Huron with Lake Michigan are four miles wide with craggy shores and islands guarding both approaches. The elevation of both bodies of water is 581 feet. Experts say this is really just one big lake with two lobes and a deep narrowing.

The state of Michigan stretches on both sides of the Mackinac Straits but it has not always been so. In the eighteenth century, the area was governed first by the French and then the British. After the English flags finally came down in 1814, the territory of Michigan was expanded to temporarily include Wisconsin, and Minnesota. In 1835, Michigan applied for statehood but its borders excluded the Upper Peninsula for being too removed and wild. A year later, however, Ohio confiscated a slice of eastern Michigan. A war between the two states was narrowly averted and Congress added the Upper Peninsula as "compensation" to Michigan.

Fierce winds were blowing torrents of rain when the *Phoenix* passed through the straits late in the afternoon on Tuesday, November 16th. It was nearly dark even though there was still half an hour before sunset. During the previous few hours, the ship had been partly shielded from the storm by the shoreline and the islands. With each mile away from the strait, the waves grew larger and larger. Big waves smashed several cabin portholes. Some of the equipment fastened on the deck was smashed and washed away.

For over an hour, the ship battled the seas until, finally, 13-mile long Beaver Island partially shielded them from the wind. Mr. Watts consulted with the captain who then ordered the ship to be anchored on the lee side of the island. A tour to inspect the damage followed. The broken cabin portholes were hastily boarded while most other repairs were left until daytime.

With the most pressing tasks completed, Mr. Watts went on to give a full situation report to the captain in his cabin. The ship was safely anchored and the remaining repairs were to be completed in the morning. The *Phoenix* could resume the journey the following afternoon providing the weather would improve. There was barely enough fuel to reach Sheboygan

The captain regretted that his bad knee was preventing him from inspecting the ship. He was concerned about the delay but there were times when schedules had to be disregarded.

Sheboygan was 200 miles away and the repairs needed to be finished before the ship could sail again. Hopefully, during the night, the storm would spend the worst of its fury.

Instead of diminishing, the storm grew still stronger. Wednesday morning, the skies remained dark. Fierce winds were blowing over the island and only a couple of cabins were visible ashore. The ship was riding hard at anchor but at least the island shielded it from the worst waves.

The rest of the day remained dark with rain and howling winds pummeling the sides of the cabins. The crewmen finished the most urgent repairs but the first mate was reluctant to get underway. He discussed with the captain his concerns about Sheboygan having no harbor. It would be impossible to dock at the open-water pier in bad weather. It was better to remain anchored, partially shielded by Beaver Island, and wait for the storm to subside. The captain reluctantly agreed.

On Thursday morning, the storm continued unabated. Hours passed as the first mate waited in vain for some improvement. Finally, Mr. Watts consulted the captain who agreed to stay anchored for another night.

The delay was testing the captain's patience. "We must leave tomorrow morning, regardless of the weather. Each day we are using up wood and have barely enough fuel to cross Lake Michigan. I think we should head for Manitowoc since it is 25 miles closer than Sheboygan. If the storm does not subside, we will anchor off Manitowoc and wait there for the conditions to improve."

Mr. Watts was surprised by the change in destination. There was some cargo to be dropped off in Manitowoc. The original plan, however, was to unload that merchandise on the return leg of the journey. "Captain, I thought that your priority would be to minimize the delay for the passengers getting off in Sheboygan and other destinations. The extra stopover will be adding to that delay."

Captain Sweet shook his head. "If this gale continues, we will not be able to dock at the open-water pier in Sheboygan. There is no harbor at either port but Manitowoc's shoreline is curved and offers more protection from prevailing winds. We need more fuel and will have a better chance to dock in Manitowoc."

Mr. Watts readily agreed; quite content to let the captain make the tough decisions. The ship was running behind schedule and the first mate did not want to be blamed for the delay. For someone aspiring to become a captain, it was important to be cooperative and maintain a good record.

The storm did ease off somewhat Friday morning. The sky was still dark gray but the howling wind was not as fierce. The deck hands had a hard time raising the anchor, which had become firmly implanted in the lake bottom. The ship had to maneuver forward and back several times before the anchor was finally freed. The *Phoenix* soon cleared the island and started the long dash across Lake Michigan. There was no need to worry about a collision with a fishing boat or a sailing ship. Only the newest steamships would brave open waters in weather like that.

No hot dishes were available for lunch in the dining room. At least the bread was still relatively fresh and served with the finest hams. Tisdale, the cabin boy, was busy refilling hot coffee and tea at the two tables. The diners had to hold on to the cups as anything loose would slide off the table. Still, the passengers lingered in the dining room, seeking the company of others. Mr. Watts informed the group about the Manitowoc stopover. The Hazelton sisters gave an update on their visit with the captain. Captain Sweet's knee remained swollen but the pain had subsided and he was in good spirits.

For the steerage passengers, the storm meant confinement

in the crowded cargo compartment. Their rations were bread and sausage, with no hot drinks available. Hours passed, the dark compartment filled with children's cries. The air was stuffy and the passengers, especially those close to the boiler room, took off all heavy clothing.

By evening, the storm had eased off somewhat. The cooks served cutlets and other simple fried dishes in the dining room. Mr. Watts gave an update, estimating they would arrive in Manitowoc around noon the following day. Weather permitting, they would refuel and sail during the night to Sheboygan. The Hazelton sisters were particularly thrilled at the prospect of spending Sunday with their parents. They urged the other passengers to go ashore in Sheboygan and visit their parents' hotel.

Outside, the night was pitch-black with no stars or lights visible anywhere. The ship lurched and rolled and most passengers lay awake thinking about their destinations. A sense of resolve pervaded the immigrants in the steerage compartment. They had survived the transatlantic passage and they would also survive the final trying days of this journey.

The lack of fresh air was the biggest problem in the steerage compartment. Several times during the day and evening, the immigrants opened the hatch even though the gale blew cold rain inside and wetted the bedding of those near the opening. The families huddled together and the tired passengers alternated between stretches of sleep and wakeful tossing. Some children cried. They were not comforted by the assurances that they had only two more nights left on the ship.

A little girl whispered. "Where are we going to sleep when we buy our land in Wisconsin?"

Her father patiently explained, "At first we will sleep in a "lean-to" shelter made out of tree branches. Within a few weeks, we will build a small log cabin. At night we will keep a bright fire so everybody can be warm."

The girl's mother then took over, describing how she would prepare pancakes and other delicious meals. The brother chipped in, stating that he would hunt in the woods and bring back rabbits and deer. In a few days, they would reach their new homesteads in Wisconsin and life was going to be wonderful.

The whole night, the *Phoenix* rolled and lurched as she sailed toward Manitowoc. Saturday morning came and the dark gray skies became visible again. The storm seemed to have grown in intensity again. The ship was tossed by the waves but plowed steadily ahead. The *Phoenix* was like a horse that could sense a rest place was near and would plod ahead without any prompting.

Shortly before noon the wheelsman spotted Manitowoc's lighthouse through the rain. An hour passed before they got close enough to recognize the hotel at the end of the pier and the entrance to the river. The shores were pounded by large waves and the ship rolled widely in its initial approach to the pier. Turning the *Phoenix* around, Mr. Watts ordered the anchor dropped to await a break in the weather. The first mate was not going to risk damaging the ship during docking or possibly wrecking the fragile pier.

Two hours passed while the *Phoenix* passengers could only watch the tiny settlement. There were only a few dozen dwellings in Manitowoc, most of them small cabins. Stretches of forest were visible just beyond the buildings.

Gradually, the storm was losing its fury although the anchored ship was still tossed by the waves. At 3:30 PM, the captain knew that a deadline was approaching fast. In two hours, it would be dark. He did not want the *Phoenix* to remain anchored overnight; they had to approach the pier in daylight.

The anchor was raised and the steam horn was sounded to alert the pier official. Gingerly the first mate steered the ship for the pier. A line was expertly thrown, catching the protruding pillar. With her forward momentum restrained by the line, the *Phoenix* grudgingly swung closer to the pier. The side of the ship violently rubbed against the pier, only partially protected by the fishing-net fender. A second line was thrown to secure the ship and gradually the rocking motion of the ship diminished. Soon the deckhands dragged the gangway connecting the ship to the pier. It was just after 4 PM in the afternoon.

The first mate quickly organized a work party to carry the cords of wood used to fuel the ship. It was important to select the available stock and at least start the loading while there was still some daylight left. The work party consisted of firemen, deckhands, and young immigrants who would be rewarded with cooked meals and hot soup. The hard work lasted more than two hours. Half way through, it got dark and only the lights from the hotel helped to guide the men to the pier.

Standing at the door to the hotel, the bartender waited anxiously for when the work party would finish loading the wood, "Boys, you deserve a drink and I got just what you want."

In the meantime, Mr. Watts stopped by the captain's cabin. The gale was still quite strong and the first mate recommended an overnight stopover in Manitowoc. The Manitowoc pier was partly sheltered while the one in Sheboygan was in the open and would not be accessible during a gale.

The captain knew that the crew and the passengers were near the limit of their endurance. The ship was behind schedule but one additional night could not make that much difference. Reluctantly, he agreed to the delay.

As darkness fell, the cabin passengers converged on the dining room. Hot coffee was soon available and the cooks busily prepared the first hot meal in two days. The wind was still pounding against the ship but at least the rain had stopped.

Clarence O'Connor was surprised that a steamship stopped at such a small settlement. "If we had better weather, I would have gone ashore. This is our first stop in Wisconsin and it would have been interesting to see the lifestyle here."

Eliza Hazelton warned him that streets in Manitowoc were likely to be quite similar to Sheboygan. "The streets are full of mud after any rain. You need high boots to walk around and, in some places, you may get stuck and not be able to pull your boots out."

David Blish laughed, listening to the wisdom dispensed by this teenage girl. He was also considering visiting the local general store to check out the hardware selection and the prices. It certainly would have been difficult to avoid mud holes.

The ship's barkeeper was busy in the dining room as passengers ordered drinks to celebrate the safe arrival in port. The cook started to serve appetizers. The main meal would take more time but in the meantime the dining room was filled with a festive atmosphere. Toasts were frequent and effusive.

David Blish raised his glass, "To our captain and the faithful first mate who have brought us safely across three great lakes and through the worst of storms."

A few minutes later, Blish grabbed a bottle of whiskey and walked to the captain's quarters. The Hazelton sisters followed him with their own glasses of cider and they all toasted the master of the ship. The girls started to sing their favorite song about the Shenandoah River. Other passengers followed by singing other songs outside the cabin.

Afterward, Blish asked Captain Sweet if they would remain in Manitowoc until the morning. The captain shook his head. "No, we are too far behind schedule and I feel that this gale will soon weaken. I am planning to remain here till 1 AM, which means the *Phoenix* will arrive in Sheboygan early Sunday morning. If we leave Sheboygan by 8 AM, the *Phoenix* will arrive in Chicago Monday night."

Blish raised his glass. "Sounds fine to me. I am looking forward to get to Southport tomorrow night and see my family again."

In the steerage compartment, there were no intoxicating drinks to celebrate the safe arrival in port. Instead, most of the women and children remained topside to watch their men carrying wood. There was no more rain but the wind was fierce and cold. Manitowoc, their first Wisconsin port, was a disappointment. There were only about thirty buildings in sight and most of them were crude shacks. Dense stretches of woods could be seen in every direction. It was surprising that such a small settlement had a lighthouse and a pier for big steamships. Soon hot coffee was offered to the steerage passengers and most immigrants went back to their compartment.

Four young couples remained on the deck, determined to spend a few private moments together. They were already in Wisconsin and soon the Dutch group would start separating. A number of families were getting off in Sheboygan to join the county's Dutch community. About half of the remaining Hollanders bought tickets to Chicago from where they would travel either to Van Raalte's Seceder colony in southern Michigan or to the Dutch settlement in Pella, Iowa. The rest bought tickets to Milwaukee and would buy land somewhere in Wisconsin. Their destinations were not firmly fixed, however. Many of the undecided Hollanders would consider staying in Sheboygan if the area looked prosperous. Even more persuasive would be an appearance at the pier of a Dutch-speaking settler.

Two of the young couples had been engaged back in Holland and their families had vowed to travel and buy land together. The other two couples had first met during the transatlantic journey. Their courtship was intense though they were careful not to be seen spending much time together. The girls' families had tickets to Milwaukee, as did the family of one of the courting boys. The other boy's family was going to Michigan. The boy first begged his father to settle in Wisconsin and then threatened to stay there on his own. The father declared that his son's duty was to build the family cabin and help with the first harvest. The boy was still hoping to convince his parents to settle in Wisconsin; otherwise, he promised his sweetheart to join her the following year.

Right after 7 PM, the work party had carried the last load of wood. The lights in the nearby tavern beckoned the crewmen just like flames would attract moths. The first mate went to the captain's cabin with a report. "The wood restocking has been completed. The winds are still quite strong and I recommend that we remain in Manitowoc until tomorrow."

Captain Sweet merely replied that he expected the gale to weaken soon.

Returning to deck, Mr. Watts found that half of the crew was already celebrating at the hotel's saloon. It was annoying but the first mate knew that it would be impossible to confine all crewmen aboard the ship. It was a tough journey and the seamen deserved a chance to unwind. Considering the weather, the first mate was fairly certain that the *Phoenix* would remain in port until morning. The men were bound to get drunk but at least they would have the rest of the night to sleep it off. Several deck hands and one fireman in the boiler room were standing watch and, thus, would remain sober.

It was still possible that the captain could order the *Phoenix's* departure during the night, if weather improved. The first mate decided that, in two hours, he would go to the saloon and order the sailors back to the ship. His only leverage was to threaten them with a suspension of the 'end-of-the-shipping-season' bonus. There was a danger, however, that they would choose to forego the bonus and continue drinking.

At the saloon, the *Phoenix* crewmen ordered a bottle of whiskey as soon as they walked in. Around the table the men relaxed, still sweaty from hard labor. The bartender brought out strong dark beer to serve both as a chaser and as a form of nourishment.

John Nugent, first fireman, quizzed his mates, the two Canadian deckhands. "Tell me, are you planning to come back in the spring?"

John Murdock scoffed. "My fiancée wants me to buy a farm and settle down. I guess I am ready to do just that, especially after this stormy passage."

John's younger brother, August Murdock, lacked the money or interest to buy a farm. His girl friend lived in Cleveland so he was definitely planning to come back.

Another deckhand in the group was Thomas Fortui from the River St. Clair settlement. Being single, with lots of girlfriends, he was always broke. He liked the *Phoenix*, especially the ship's food. and thus was also planning to come back.

John Nugent, the first fireman, was the only married man, with a wife and two children living in Buffalo. Working in the boiler room was a hard job but at least he had free time during the winter to spend time with his family. He said that he had been with the *Phoenix* since her launch and planned to remain for as long as she would sail.

"We'll drink to that," his companions answered with another toast.

Chapter 16

Manitowoc - Lake Michigan

Manitowoc in 1853, Manitowoc County Historical Society

At 9 PM, Saturday, November 20th, only a handful of lights still flickered in Manitowoc. This tiny settlement of less than one hundred inhabitants would expand in just eight years to a population of thirteen thousand. The first locally built sailing ship was launched in 1847 and soon the community became known for shipyards. During World War II, twenty-eight US Navy submarines were built in Manitowoc. The challenge was how to get the submarines, which required twelve feet of draft, to the ocean. The only way was through the Illinois and Mississippi Rivers where some sections were only nine feet deep. The Manitowoc's solution was to transport the submarines on a dry-dock barge, which reduced the overall draft to only five feet.

As the evening passed, the gale was slowly subsiding. Mr. Watts went to confer with Captain Sweet about the next day's schedule. To his surprise, the captain insisted on departing from Manitowoc at 1 AM. Captain Sweet wanted to arrive in Sheboygan at dawn, continue to Milwaukee, and reach Southport by the end of Sunday. After one more stopover at Littleport, the *Phoenix* would finally arrive in Chicago Monday night.

After leaving the captain's cabin, the first mate first action was to get all the crewmen aboard. As he entered the saloon, Mr. Watts was dismayed to see that most of his crewmen were slumped in a drunken stupor. John Nugent, the usually reliable first fireman, shakily grabbed a bottle and offered it to the first mate.

Mr. Watts announced loudly, "The Phoenix is leaving in a few hours and its time to get back to the ship."

The crewmen were in no condition to resist the first mate's order. They helped each other stand up and slowly staggered back to the ship. There would not be much time to sober up before departure.

Once aboard, it was difficult for John Nugent to negotiate the ladder down to his workstation. He passed by the boiler, attended by Michael O'Brien, and growled that he was to be awakened just before the ship would get underway. After a few more steps, Nugent slumped in a corner, his head resting on his knees.

In the dining room, a few of the cabin passengers still lingered over drinks. The women had all retired so the men did not need to watch their language or avoid risqué subjects. The stormy passage and the drinks made them tipsy, however. Hearing from Mr. Watts that they would arrive in Sheboygan at dawn, the men eventually retired for the night. Early in the morning they would be up to say good-bye to the Hazelton sisters and to catch a glimpse of the community.

Eliza and Anne Hazelton stayed wide-awake in their cabin, anxious to know whether the ship would depart that night. Huddled in a narrow bunk, the two sisters discussed all the stories they would tell their parents upon arrival. They discussed the things they had missed most about home: being comforted by mother and listening to father's tales, never certain whether they were true or just wild exaggerations. Eliza was worried, nonetheless, that her mother would criticize them for not persevering in the boarding school. Anne reassured her older sister that father would not allow any criticism to spoil the homecoming. Christmas was near and it was only right for family to be together.

Outside the wind continued to grow weaker. In the southerly direction, a section of the moon briefly appeared before being covered by the clouds again. Shortly after 1 AM, the lines were hauled in and the ship moved out into the open waters. Once again part of the moon reappeared. The *Phoenix* steamed straight toward the shining moon, like a moth speeding toward a flame.

Once out on the lake, the ship started to roll again but it was nowhere near as severe as during the previous night. Most of the passengers woke up initially, disturbed by the machinery noise and the vibration of the twin-screw shafts. The gentle rocking of the ship soon eased most of the passengers back to sleep. Filled with anticipation, the Hazelton sisters remained awake seemingly for hours before they too finally fell into a deep sleep.

Meanwhile, the engine room was bursting with activity. The first mate's order called for maximum power and both firemen were busy shoving the logs into the boiler furnace. Nugent was groggy but was loading wood almost as quickly as O'Brien.

The faster they got to Sheboygan, the sooner he could get a bit of rest. Mr. House, the engineer, remained in the engine room for over an hour. They were steaming as quickly as could be expected with the ship's heavy load. Eventually Mr. House decided to get some sleep. The second engineer would handle the engine room until they got close to Sheboygan.

In the pilothouse, the first mate scanned the skies and was amazed by the break in weather. After nine stormy days, the wind calmed down and the waves turned into gentle rollers. The only white foam was where the ship's bow was slicing through the water. Outside the pilothouse's window, a few snowflakes could be seen floating down, a sign of an early winter. After a while, Mr. Watts turned over the watch to the second mate. The first mate would resume the control just before they arrived at port. Sunday was going to be a busy day.

In the cabin passenger section, only a few gentle snores emanated from the compartments. At some point, something disturbed Clarence O'Connor and he became awake, at first confused where he was. The gentle rolling spurred him to recall the previous evening's celebration of the ship's safe arrival in Manitowoc. The dinner was delicious and included in the cost of the ticket; the drinks were excellent but expensive. They had to watch their expenses, so O'Connor limited himself to only one drink. He lay in silence for several minutes trying to rationalize what was keeping him awake. His stomach felt bloated from too much food but there was something else that kept him wary.

Finally it hit him. It was that faint whistling sound, which he could barely pick out between the rhythmic banging of the pistons and the distant grinding of the screw shafts. The same sound that two years earlier had disturbed him when he was working in the knitting mill in Ireland. At that time, O'Connor alerted the chief mechanic who explained afterwards that the boiler was low on water. At any moment the superheated steam could cause a boiler explosion.

O'Connor immediately got dressed, ran to the boiler-room's hatch, and descended down the ladder. The whistling sound was more pronounced there but nobody paid any attention to it. He approached the nearest man.

"Your boiler is low on water and soon it's going to explode."

The man looked groggy and hostile. His reply was curt. "Who the hell are you?"

O'Connor rushed through the explanation. "I have worked as a boiler engineer in a knitting mill in Ireland. I just woke up and became aware of this strange whistling hum. It is the sound of the superheated steam, which will result in an explosion unless you immediately add water to the boiler."

The fireman stammered. "We already have one smart-arse Irish fireman on this ship. Now a smart-arse knitting engineer wants to take over as the ship's engineer. I suggest that you leave the ship's affairs to those who run the ships. Now get out of here."

O'Connor tried to get past the inebriated fireman but was hit by a punch that made him stagger back. Slowly he started to climb the ladder while calling out to the other men in the boiler-room. "The boiler is short of water; it is going to explode at any moment."

William Owen, the second engineer, called to Nugent to leave the Irishman alone. Afterward he went to the boiler water valve and made sure it was fully turned on. He then turned a second valve and kept it in the on position for over a minute. There was little change in the cacophony of the clanking pistons, the grinding of the screw shafts, and the rhythmic hissing of the released steam. The machinery sounded a bit different than usual but then they had orders to run at full steam.

Once back on deck, O'Connor looked toward the shore but

could only see darkness. He walked to the pilothouse and described the confrontation in the boiler-room. The ship needed to get as close as possible to land.

The second mate tried hard not to show his annoyance. "Mr. O'Connor, I am sure that the ship engineer is more familiar with his machinery than you are. As for our course, I have to follow the first mate's instructions. It really would be best if you simply go back to your cabin and get some sleep. We will arrive in Sheboygan at dawn."

O'Connor returned to his cabin but only to wake up his wife and daughter. They got dressed quickly, hid their valuables in their clothing, and filled a handbag with necessities. Outside, O'Connor guided his family to the nearest lifeboat. Removing the boat cover, he helped his wife and daughter get inside. Minutes passed while they awaited the boiler explosion.

Mrs. O'Connor had always been proud of her husband's boiler expertise. This time she was hoping that the catastrophe would somehow be avoided. "Perhaps the American machinery is different and the ship can sail another few hours and reach Sheboygan."

In the steerage compartment the immigrants were snoring, lulled by the gentle rocking of the ship. After many nights of being tossed around in the stormy weather, most of them fell into a deep sleep. One man lying close to the ship's funnel woke up sweaty and took off his jacket. It seemed much warmer than usual in the compartment, even though the hatch was partly opened for ventilation.

Twenty minutes later, O'Brien spotted a thin curl of gray smoke rising from the back of the boiler. He went to investigate and found a smoldering cord of dried-out wood. Small flames were visible on the edge of the logs. O'Brien shouted "fire!"

as he grabbed a bucket and opened the drain valve. For some reason the water flow was only a trickle.

Mr. Owen quickly inspected the smoking cord of wood, then returned and grabbed the partially filled bucket. O'Brien shouted that he was going topside to wake up the engineer, Mr. House.

The second engineer yelled back, "Not now, it's only a cord of wood smoldering and we will quickly put it out."

The first partially filled bucket of water generated only more smoke and a cloud of steam. Mr. Owen then sent O'Brien to get more buckets and organize deckhands to haul water straight from the lake. Several crucial minutes passed before the buckets of water were lowered into the engine room. They were losing the fight with the fire, as smoke and flames engulfed more cords of wood.

Minutes later, Mr. House appeared at the hatch. The boiler-room was already filled with smoke while Mr. Owen and Nugent kept shouting for faster water bucket delivery. The engineer barked to the deckhands to get all available hands and then ran to the pilothouse, shouting instructions to the wheelsman. "Fire in the boiler-room; turn the ship immediately toward the land." The second mate nodded his head in agreement and started to blow the steam whistle to alert all the passengers to the emergency.

Clarence O'Connor climbed down from the lifeboat and rushed toward the smoke-filled opening to the boiler-room. Joining the line of sailors, he started to pass the water buckets. Moments later David Blish appeared on the scene. He knew immediately that more hands were needed to form additional bucket brigades. There were plenty of immigrants on the ship and Blish headed for the steerage compartment to organize Dutch volunteers.

For several minutes, the buckets were lowered, emptied,

and quickly pulled out, one right after another. The hatch to the boiler-room was quickly engulfed by smoke. It was hard to imagine that the two men at the bottom were still able to grab the buckets and pour it on the burning wood stacks. Another bucket was lowered but halfway through it hit something and tipped over. The sailor at the top of the hatch shouted, "Somebody is climbing the ladder. Pour more buckets down the hatch to cool him off."

Moments later, a darkened head appeared in the hatch opening, smoke rising from the man's hair. The sailors immediately grabbed Nugent's shoulders and pulled him up on deck. More water was poured down the hatch to help Mr. Owen climb up the ladder. After an agonizing delay, the second engineer's head rose among the smoke and then slumped over the top ladder step. The sailors pulled Mr. Owen out and placed him down next to the first fireman.

Both men lay slumped on the deck. Mr. Owen was unconscious and barely breathing. Nugent was gulping the air, his eyes still shut in terror.

Mr. House leaned over Nugent and asked him what was the situation down below. Nugent briefly opened one eye then whispered, "Mr. Owen, we have to get out of here or we'll die."

The heroic struggle of the two men in the boiler-room did not provide salvation for the rest of the crew and passengers. Earlier the steam engine was running rapidly, almost in a runaway condition. Just before the men emerged from the boiler-room, the engine started to slow down. Mr. House tried one more time to find out from Nugent as to why the boiler was losing steam so quickly. Nugent's mind appeared to be still obsessed by the terror below the deck. He again repeated, "Mr. Owen, we have to get out of here or we'll die."

The first engineer looked into the darkness vainly trying to discern the shore. The *Phoenix* was rapidly losing speed; it was doubtful that they would be able to beach her. By then flames were shooting out of the boiler-room hatch and the ventilation openings. The fire had also spread to the steerage compartment. A crowd of immigrants was standing on the top deck, most of them still dressed in nightclothes.

It was clear, however, that a lot of steerage passengers were still in their compartment below the deck. Some remained, confused by the smoke and the darkness. Other women and children were probably waiting for their men to return from the bucket brigade duties. One after another, the anxious immigrants dropped the water buckets and started to seek out their families among those on the deck. Several men peered fearfully into the smoke filled steerage compartment from the deck above.

Blish was aghast, realizing that he had recruited immigrants as volunteers but failed to insure a safe evacuation for their families. He pushed aside Mr. House who tried to prevent him from going down the ladder..

Mr. House shouted a final piece of advice as Blish was descending down the ladder. "Your only chance is to crawl or stay as low as you can. The air just above the deck is cooler and contains less smoke!"

Blish dropped to the deck and paused to get used to the darkness. "Children, " he yelled in Dutch trying to find out where were the survivors.

Voices and coughing sounds came from several directions. Close to him, a child alternated between sobbing and coughing, the later an instinctive attempt to clear smoke from the lungs. Blish crawled until he reached the sobbing girl, her brother, and the mother. Unbuttoning his coat, he inserted the little boy inside. He then placed the girl's and her mother's hands on his coat and started to crawl back to the ladder.

The girl and her mother held on to Blish's coat, following

him as he crawled toward the faint light of the hatch. Reaching the ladder, Blish grabbed the girl in his right arm and quickly ascended to the top deck. Once there, he sighed with relief, seeing that the mother's head also emerged from the hold. Right behind her appeared a man, his wife, and their three children. Lost and dazed in the darkness, the other family regained their senses and followed Blish to the ladder.

For almost a minute, Blish breathed deeply to build up his strength and courage to descend below the deck again. Finally, he rushed down and again shouted "children" in Dutch. More faint voices and coughing could be heard from some distance away. He crawled toward another sobbing girl, feeling increasing heat and smoke along the way. Inserting the child inside his coat, he crawled back to the ladder and climbed out. Her parents, another sister, and two brothers followed Blish. A minute later, he again descended down into the steerage compartment, returning with another small girl.

The deck was full of frantic adults and sobbing children. Coughing and gasping, Blish forced himself back towards the steerage compartment. "Children" he cried out in Dutch again, and then coughed, his throat sore and hoarse from the smoke. He shouted two more times but there was no answer. The smoke was overpowering and his head was dizzy. Holding his breath and with closed eyes, he started to climb the ladder. Finally, his head was above the deck. He started to breathe but was totally spent and could not make another move.

As other passengers were pulling him out, the dazed Blish whispered. "I need to rest a bit before I'll try again. I know there are still more Hollanders in that compartment but they no longer answer my call...."

Chapter 17

Dead in the Water

Pheonix, by William J. Koelpin
www.americansportingarts.com

By 4:45 AM Sunday morning, the *Phoenix* had lost all speed and was dead in the water. It was November 21st, nearly ten days since the ship had departed from Buffalo, New York. The top deck was engulfed in smoke and flames. Some deckhands and passengers still kept up bucket brigades, pouring water on the deck to protect their immediate area from flames. The shoreline was not yet visible in the darkness but surely the land had to be near. It was high time to launch the lifeboats. Several back-and-forth trips would be required to evacuate all passengers.

Panic swept the ship as soon as the deckhands left the

bucket brigades to start launching the boats. Only twenty people could fit into a lifeboat and a horde surrounded each launching area on the sides of the ship and the stern. The crewmen kept shouting that the priority on the initial trip was for the cabin passengers. The Dutch immigrants did not understand what was being said and refused to stand back.

David Blish had finally recovered from the dizziness due to crawling in the smoke-filled steerage compartment. He looked around and was appalled by the frenzy of the crowd. His immediate concern was Captain Sweet who had been immobilized with his knee and could end up being left behind. Blish rushed to the captain's cabin but found it empty. Returning back to the top deck, he finally found the captain at the launching site of one of the lifeboats. The boat was already in the water. The captain was trying to keep an orderly embarkation of the lifeboat.

"Mr. Blish, cabin passengers have priority; please step into the lifeboat."

Blish shook his head stating that it was more important to get the injured captain in the lifeboat. "Right now with the help of the crewmen, we can safely lower you into the lifeboat. Later people will be jumping into the water and pulled into the boat. That would not be good for your injured knee."

The captain protested that he needed to remain aboard to insure the safe evacuation of all personnel but Blish persisted.

"With your bad knee, you would not be of much help aboard the ship. You simply can't afford to risk any additional injury to your knee. Don't worry about us. Worst come to worst, we will build some rafts and paddle to the shore."

The captain reluctantly agreed to be lowered into the lifeboat. Once again he implored Blish to also take a seat in the lifeboat.

Blish shook his head. "There is work left for me here, and

I want to take my chances with the rest."

With the captain no longer blocking the way, a scramble developed for the remaining lifeboat seats. The Dutch immigrants jumped into the boat, some falling into the water. A little girl was left behind with the rest of her family already in the boat. Blish picked her up and passed her over the heads of other passengers. She was thrown into the lifeboat into the arms of her older sister.

Some of the cabin passengers ended up at the lifeboat-boarding site at the stern where Newell Merill was in charge. The second mate succeeded in seating half a dozen of the cabin passengers in the boat. As soon as he and the two crewmen took their positions in the boat, the frantic steerage passengers started to jump, some of them dropping right on top of the other passengers. The lifeboat was heavily overloaded and low in the water. As it started to pull away from the ship, more Hollanders jumped into the water and grabbed the sides of the boat. The two crewmen rowed hard to get away but by then water was pouring in and the boat was settling down.

The burning ship illuminated the grotesque view of the cluster of human upper bodies miraculously rising above the water. A faint outline of the sinking lifeboat was barely visible at the surface. There was only one chance for the lifeboat occupants. Most of them would have to temporarily get out of the boat. This would make it possible for the others to bail the water out.

A crowd was pressing on the boarding area of the third and final lifeboat. In the middle of the crowd was Gerrit Geerlings with his family. Gerrit Koffer, the elder from Winterswijk, recognized the ex-deacon and yelled in his loudest voice, "Countrymen, make room for deacon Geerlings; we must make sure that our deacon gets safely in the lifeboat." The men parted and Geerlings stepped forward. His wife followed him but kept glancing frantically behind her. "Two of our children are not here and we can't leave without them."

The first mate recognized that the Hollanders considered this family very important and allowed Geerlings to board the lifeboat. He did not understand Dutch and simply gave the hesitant Mrs. Geerlings a shove to hurry her up. Afterwards, two more families surged forward to board the boat. Another Hollander was pushing his way with his family. The first mate let the man and his children through but stopped the large stout wife.

"You are too fat. The lifeboat is full and we will have to come back for you and the others."

Afterwards, the first mate lowered himself into the boat and immediately pushed away. A few more Hollanders managed to jump into the boat and several others ended up in the water. The passengers pulled one young woman into the lifeboat while another hung desperately to the side of the boat.

The crewmen searched for the oars but found there was only one in the boat. It was impossible to try to return to the ship, as more passengers would jump in and overload the boat. They would have to find a board in the water to use as an oar. Among the many objects thrown from the ship, Derk Voskuil fished out of the water a broom, easier to use as an oar than a board.

The oar-broom combination, and the woman hanging to the side, meant the lifeboat was moving very slowly. Mr. Watts felt the situation was jeopardizing a speedy return to save the rest of the passengers. There were already twenty-one people in the boat. He issued an order to push the woman away. A sailor loosened the Dutch woman's grip on the lifeboat and shoved her away. Gasping, she briefly reappeared on the surface but was too much in shock from the freezing water to reach the boat again.

The lifeboats were leaking as no emergency drills or maintenance had ever been carried out. Soon Mr. Watt's boat was so low in the water that some waves washed over the side. There were no buckets in the boat but fortunately the Hollanders came up with a remedy. Taking off their wooden shoes, they used them to scoop up the water and empty it over the side.

The captain's boat had two oars but was more heavily overloaded, with twenty-two people. At the stern, a woman hung desperately to the rudder, apparently unnoticed by anybody. Slowly their distance from the burning ship increased but ahead of them they still could see only darkness.

Aboard the ship, the fire intensified and there was a growing realization that the lifeboats would not return in time to save the rest of the passengers. There was still one hope left. Far away they could see the light of the Sheboygan lighthouse. Somebody was bound to see the burning ship and send help. The flames were spreading fast, however. They would not be able to stay much longer aboard the ship.

Rafts could save lives of those forced to jump into the water. Grabbing a broadax, Mr. House started to knock down doors and the sides of the passengers' cabins. Blish entered the smoke-filled cabins to grab chairs and anything that could float. Boards and all floatable items were thrown in the water to form rafts.

The water was freezing and most passengers wanted to stay on the ship for as long as possible. Two separate throngs formed at the bow and the stern of the ship. Those on the outside screamed as the flames burned their legs and scorched their clothes. Several men climbed the mast and tied themselves to a spar to keep from falling. Soon the deck below them was totally ablaze and the bursting flames were getting close to them.

As time passed, more and more of the passengers escaped

the flames and smoke by jumping into the lake. One couple, to be married upon arrival in Wisconsin, held hands and jumped into the water. Another young couple kissed each other for the first time since they had first met in Rotterdam. Then, still embracing, they slipped into the water. The boy reappeared on the surface and towed his girlfriend to a nearby floating door. They partly pulled themselves out of the water. The girl first smiled but then started to shake uncontrollably from the shock of the cold water.

Soon the flames reached the two Hazelton sisters who had been late getting out of their cabin and missed the lifeboat boarding. Stealthily the flames were creeping up closer and closer, occasionally bursting out with stings of terror like a coiled snake intimidating its victim.

The two sisters looked anxiously in the southerly direction. Just beyond the lighthouse, there was a faint light, which probably came from their father's hotel. Vainly, the girls watched for a sign of rescue coming from Sheboygan. Soon the edges of Eliza's dress were on fire and the two sisters clasped their hands and jumped into the water. Only the tops of their heads briefly reappeared, their hair spread in the water like clumps of sea grass. Then the sisters submerged forever as if conscripted to Neptune's court of mermaids.

Two families from Racine and Milwaukee remained at the stern of the ship. Edwin West had earlier thrown overboard some material to build a raft for his wife and their child. His wife was scared they would become separated in the water so they all joined hands and jumped together. They came up to the surface but the float was too far away and they perished.

The terrified Milwaukee family still remained at the stern. Moments later the flames ignited the bottom of Mrs. Long's dress. She shrieked and jumped into the water, her child embraced in her arms. Mr. Long paused just long enough to see where they would reappear. To his horror, they were nowhere in sight. He finally jumped, no longer caring whether he would survive.

Mr. House stopped knocking down the cabin walls and used his broadax to cut a fender rope. Using that as a float, he jumped into the water and swam to a nearby floating door. Fastening the fender and the door, he partially pulled himself out of the water and looked around. All around him were drifting objects and people clinging to anything floatable.

A handful of frightened Dutch immigrants remained on the ship. The heroic David Blish was among them, his clothes burnt and his hair singed. In his arms he was shielding a shocked little Dutch girl while gesturing to the rest of her family to leap into the water. Once again the flames exploded and finally everybody jumped overboard. Blish reappeared at the surface, still holding the girl, and swam toward some wooden pieces floating nearby. He scurried to fashion a raft and place the girl above the water. He asked her for her name and then shouted it loudly, trying to attract the attention of the rest of her family. Many immigrants were floating nearby but nobody answered to his call. Blish was shivering and started to enlarge the raft so he could pull himself above the water.

"Mr. Blish, " a voice called from behind him.

David Blish turned his head and recognized his favorite Dutch pupil, Jan Koffers. The boy was floating on a log with his sister, perhaps twenty feet away.

"Wisconsin, the home of the brave. You went into the smoke and fire to save Hollanders. You more brave than anybody else...."

Blish shouted to his friend that they would build a raft together. Slowly he started to swim and push his raft toward the Koffers children. Jan and his siblings were totally numb and could barely cling to their log. Blish knew he had to build a bigger raft quickly before he too slipped into stupor.

All around were dozens of passengers clinging to anything that could float. The temperature was near the freezing point and a light snow started to fall. Those with only their heads above the water were soon too numb to cry for help. Horace Tisdale, the cabin boy, was barely afloat when he spotted something sticking out of the water. With a great effort he maneuvered to get himself prone on top of a ladder. He was partially out of the water, with improved chances for survival. There was still no sight of the shore but the lifeboats were bound to be returning soon.

By then, the whole deck of the *Phoenix* was ablaze and huge flames shot up from the openings in the sides of the ship. The fire was raging at the base of the mast where earlier several men had tied themselves to the spar high above the deck. Mr. House, shivering on top a floating door, watched in horror as the mast toppled right into the blazing inferno on the deck. He wondered whether the men who toppled with the mast, were still alive or had succumbed to smoke earlier.

Chapter 18

Sheboygan

Sheboygan, the first white settlement, 1834,
Sheboygan County Research Center

In 1847, Sheboygan was still without a harbor. The Sheboygan River was not dredged and often blocked by sand bars. A long pier sticking into Lake Michigan provided the only maritime access but only in fair weather. On Saturday, November 20th, the lake was too rough for docking and two ships ended up anchoring near the river. One was the two-masted schooner *Liberty* and the other a small steamship *Delaware*.

The later ship was a small propeller steamship traveling from Milwaukee. At first, Captain Tuttle of the *Delaware* had decided to skip Sheboygan and proceed to Manitowoc. He had to reconsider, however, due to the strong protest from the

Sheboygan-bound passengers led by Mr. C.B. Dawley, a well-known pioneer farmer.

Shortly after the start of the mid watch, from four to eight in the morning, a sailor aboard the *Liberty* noticed a distant light to the north. At first he thought it was some fisherman but minutes passed and the red glow seemed to grow stronger. He woke up the captain and they both knew that a ship, probably a darn steamer, was on fire. Steamships were trying to put sailing ships out of business but were prone to spectacular fires occurring almost every year. Still there were sailors and passengers aboard and they had to be helped.

With practically no wind, the schooner would never be able to reach the distressed ship in time. Close to them was the propeller *Delaware* but most likely its boiler was cold. Captain Potter fired his gun and started to ring the ship's bell to alert the other ship and the residents of Sheboygan. In the meantime, preparations were started to launch the lifeboat. Soon, with steady powerful strokes, the crewmen were rowing in the race against time to save human lives.

Aboard the *Delaware*, Captain Tuttle heard the shot from the schooner and quickly got out of his cabin, only partly dressed. Minutes later, the engineer and the fireman were working furiously to stoke up the fire. The captain wondered what kind of ship was on fire. His primary concern was saving lives of fellow mariners and passengers. However, there was another powerful motive to rush to the wreck. The ship was likely to be a steamer and the equipment and the hardware cargo could generate substantial salvage proceeds if the wreck could be towed to shore.

It takes time to boil a large pot of water and even more time to generate steam in a boiler. The captain was anxiously pacing the deck waiting for the report that they were ready to sail. In the distance the red glow seemed to grow bigger and more distinct. One could only hope that there were only a few passengers traveling on that ship. The captain knew that most ships did not have enough lifeboats to carry the crew and all passengers. It was the end of the shipping season and the weather was very stormy. So hopefully few passengers had booked the passage and perhaps some cancelled at the last minute.

Minutes after the shot had been heard, Mr. Kirkland who was in charge of the pier operations, arrived at the waterfront. At first he assumed that one of the ships was preparing to tie up for unloading. He could see the dark outline of the *Delaware* but was not sure if there was smoke rising from the funnel. Then he noticed the red glow to the north and knew that somewhere close there was a ship on fire.

More Sheboygan inhabitants appeared at the pier asking questions about the distant fire and rescue plans. Soon a majority of the local population was standing on the beaches watching the distant fire. A few of the more practical men were organizing the rescue boats.

Finally, some steam was available and the *Delaware* slowly turned toward the red glow. The crewmen and passengers were on deck anxiously looking at the distant fire. After covering a mile, they were able to estimate fairly accurately the distance to the ship. The inferno was about eight miles from the pier and more than four miles from the nearest shore.

Captain Tuttle was mystified as to why the burning ship was so far away from land. The shoreline between Manitowoc and Sheboygan was curved so a ship traveling in a straight line would be several miles from shore. However, at the first sign of fire, a captain would turn his steamship toward land. In the past, most passengers from the burning ships had been able to wade from the beached ship to the shore.

With the burning ship so far from the shore, only those in the lifeboats had a chance to reach the land. Captain Tuttle knew that most people would last less than one hour in the freezing water, even if they were holding on to pieces of wood.

A long hour passed as the *Delaware* closed in on the burning ship. Mr. Dawley who had previously been so incensed by his inability to disembark in Sheboygan, was at the bow of the ship, anxiously watching the fire ahead. The *Phoenix* looked like a fiery Viking funeral vessel, with flames starting from the waterline and rising high in the air. It seemed there were still people on the ship frantically moving to and fro when suddenly the upper deck collapsed.

A number of people in the water remained alive, though numb and silent. Mr. House, on top of his floating door, was the first one to spot the lights of the approaching steamer and shouted encouragement to those around him.

"Hold on; I can see a rescue ship getting near."

A young woman was floating near Mr. House, clinging to a settee, but she was too numb to turn her head. A little bit further, Horace Tisdale, the cabin boy, lay on a ladder but he also did not react. Only one groan was heard from a man stretched on top of a log.

Another five minutes passed and then still another. The only sound around was the sizzling fire and the occasional collapse of some burnt out section aboard the ship hulk. One by one the remaining numb travelers were succumbing to hypothermia, loosening their grips, and slipping below the waves.

A new sound of splashing water was heard. Like a ghost emerging from the haze, a rowboat appeared and threaded its way through the floating pieces. Captain Potter from the schooner *Liberty* searched in vain for any sign of survivors. Then he spotted a miracle: two men hanging on to the rudder chain off the burning wreck. At first the men were too numb to provide any information. The sailors wrapped them with coats and rubbed their backs before one of the men spoke up.

"The lifeboats did not return. Everybody drowned...."

Almost at the same time, the propeller *Delaware* had entered the area of the spread-out flotsam. The ship slowed down and the sailors and passengers looked hard to spot any survivors. Mr. Dawley saw a figure on top of a small raft that showed a sign of life. A boat was quickly launched and the man was pulled inside.

"I am Mr. House, the engineer," he whispered. "I saw your lights but the others just could not hold on any longer...."

There were no other survivors in the area. It was best to return to the ship so that Mr. House could change into dry warm clothes. The lifeboat from the *Liberty* also pulled alongside the propeller and transferred their two survivors: the clerk T.S. Donahue and the cabin passenger Mr. Long from Milwaukee. Mr. Dawley took off his coat for the survivors and they were led into the dining room.

Both boats then went back to criss-cross the sections surrounding the *Phoenix*. Eight more figures were found in the water but all were dead. The most poignant was the cabin boy stretched out on the ladder, finally at eternal rest after a short life of errands.

In the meantime, Captain Tuttle was trying to decide whether there was a chance of successfully towing the burning wreck to the shore. The fire had consumed the wood practically to the waterline. Still the ship could float for quite some time and the machinery and hardware salvage proceeds would be substantial. Finally, he decided to go ahead with the salvage. Instructions were issued to attach a line to the rudder to begin the towing operation.

It seemed like a lifetime before the lifeboat commanded by Captain Sweet finally reached the shore. Many passengers wore only nightclothes and some were wet after being pulled out of the water. Everybody was freezing except for the sailors who had exhausted themselves rowing as quickly as they could. They covered over four miles in the overloaded boat and the crewmen were spent.

As soon as they got close to shore, the lifeboat passengers jumped into the water. It was at that time that a woman was discovered clinging to the rudder. She seemed to be still alive but totally numb. The distraction gave the crewmen a short moment of rest but soon they started to row back to the *Phoenix* to pick up more passengers.

Captain Sweet looked at his shivering passengers and knew the top priority was to start a fire. Fortunately there was plenty of driftwood and some men had pipes and matches in their coats. It was ironic that those shivering survivors from the burning ship were waiting so anxiously for the flames to restart again. Soon a small fire took hold and more and more wood was being thrown to make it bigger. The Dutch woman who had floated in the water behind the lifeboat, remained dazed and unresponsive. Captain Sweet kept scanning the water and the beaches around them. Did the other two lifeboats drift further away or were they simply slower?

The lifeboat commanded by Mr. Watts, the first mate, was three-quarters of the way toward the shore when they noticed the fire on the beach. The combination of one oar and the broom was not very conducive for efficient rowing. In addition, the lifeboat was overloaded and badly leaking water, with the Hollanders feverishly emptying it with their wooden shoes. The sight of the bonfire spurred the crew to row harder and finally they also reached the beach. Some of the women could hardly stand up and had to be helped to walk ashore.

The passengers from the first lifeboat rushed to the newcomers to see if any relatives were among them. Mothers cried out the names of the missing children. There were no reunited families. The anxious Hendrik Wilterdink did not find his wife, children, or his brother's family in the other lifeboat. He was startled, however, to see Willemina Ten Dolle, his family's eighteen-year old maid.

The new survivors were led to the fire. Wet coats were spread on tree branches and waved near the big bonfire. Steam drifted from the clothes while people took turns standing next to the fire. By then there was daylight but there was still no sign of the third lifeboat. In the distance they could see a rescue steamship with smoke rising from a funnel. Behind it was a faint outline of the *Phoenix*, with flames still rising above its surface. There was a growing realization that probably there were no more survivors aboard the ship's hulk or in the water. The people around the fire were dumbfounded.

There were only forty-three survivors from the ship. Four of them were the crew members from Cleveland: Captain Sweet, Mr. Watts, the first mate, second porter E. Watts, and deckhand John Mann. The other two crewmen were A.G. Kelso, wheelman, from Ohio City and fireman O'Brien from Buffalo. Also saved were Mr. and Mrs. O'Connor and their daughter plus Hamlin Heath. The steerage passengers who reached the beach consisted of twenty-five Hollanders and eight other immigrants.

All the passengers remained by the fire except for one Irish girl who stood by the waves wailing and hoping for more survivors to appear from the water. Seven other members of her family were missing. Michael O'Brien, the fireman, walked up to the girl and tried to comfort her.

"There is still another lifeboat, somewhere out there. Or perhaps your family was picked up by the rescue ship...."

Some would consider Gerrit and Eliza Geerlings to be lucky as they both survived, along with four of their children. All that Eliza could do, however, was to cry for her missing seventeen-year old son and thirteen-year old daughter.

"My father wanted us to live in Holland. God is punishing me for disobeying my father's wishes."

Standing at the fire next to Geerlings, was Jan Oonk from Winterswijk, with his three daughters. When the survivors of the two lifeboats were reunited, he vainly searched for his wife and three sons. Also missing was Jan's brother Gerrit, his wife, and two of their children. There was no sign of Jan's other niece who was traveling as a maid with the Siebelink family. The generous Hendrik Siebelink, who had helped to finance the tickets for the two Oonk families, most likely was too gentle to push his way into the lifeboats.

Even more grief-struck was Teunis Schuppert from Holten, Overijssel. His only child, a two-year-old daughter, was safe but his wife Gerdina was numb and unresponsive in his arms. She had remained in the water during the entire passage from the ship, holding on to the lifeboat's rudder. Could he have done something to force the crew to pull her to safety in the overloaded boat? Or would they push her instead into oblivion, had they been aware that she was impeding the boat's progress? He could only hope that she would recover and forgive him for not protecting her better.

Three of Gerdina's sisters were standing near to her. The recently married twenty-two year old Teuntje was hugging her husband Berend Wissink. The twenty-year-old Hendrika Landeweerd was standing near the fire trying to warm up her three-year-old sister Hanna. The sisters' parents, three brothers, and one other sister were not able to board the lifeboats and did not survive. Four Landerweerd sisters had reached the shore but only three of them were real survivors. The barely alive Gerdina never recovered and months later was the first to rejoin her departed family in the eternal world.

Chapter 19

Sheboygan II

Early Sheboygan, The Newberry Library, Chicago

The burned-out hulk of the *Phoenix* dragged behind the propeller *Delaware* like an obstinate calf being hauled away to market. The towing operation greatly reduced the *Delaware's* speed and anxious hours passed while the ship was slowly steaming toward the Sheboygan's pier. The three half-frozen survivors, Mr. House, the engineer, T.S. Donahue, the ship's clerk, and the Milwaukee passenger, Mr. Long, were warming up in the lounge. After a while the survivors started to provide more details about the fire disaster.

Captain Tuttle was astonished to hear that the *Phoenix* was carrying over two hundred steerage passengers. The total number of passengers and crew, therefore, amounted to nearly three hundred people. The lifeboats could carry only about twenty passengers each and it was questionable whether the third lifeboat had even reached the shore.

Mr. House was greatly disappointed that the heroic David

Blish had not been picked up from the water. There was still a slim chance that his raft had drifted close to the third lifeboat. That boat was last seen swamped and full of passengers who barely protruded above the water. The engineer was hopeful that, if Blish had been able to get close to that lifeboat, he would succeed in organizing its rescue. The passengers would be persuaded to temporarily evacuate the boat. Water would then be bailed out; people could get back in the lifeboat and proceed to the beach.

Captain Tuttle also received information about the hardware carried aboard the *Phoenix*. The salvage proceeds from this operation would be in the thousands of dollars, providing they could reach the shore. For the time being, the burned-out hulk refused to go down. Water splashed over the sides but immediately turned into clouds of steam. The slow journey continued.

After collecting blankets, the land rescue party from Sheboygan set off to look for any survivors on the distant beaches. North of Sheboygan, the shores were full of obstacles: first a marshy river, then a combination of forested dunes, cliffs, and creeks. At times, the rough road to the north strayed some distance away from Lake Michigan. The horse wagons and the rescuers sometimes separated from each other, determined to search all areas where lifeboats or rafts could have landed.

Time passed and the thinly dressed passengers were freezing while waiting for their turn next to the fire. Finally, some Hollanders decided to walk to Sheboygan. They followed the beaches but occasionally the cliffs were right at the water edge. In a few places, they had to jump over wet rocks or climb to the top of a cliff. Most of the Hollanders were without coats and grew quite cold. At least the exertion kept their minds focused on the road rather than on their missing relatives and friends.

Sometime before midmorning, the horse wagons had finally reached the lifeboat-landing site. Captain Sweet was placed on the wagon and covered with a sheepskin. His first question was whether they knew of any additional survivors. The men from the rescue party shook their heads. There was still hope that the third boat had landed farther away. There was also a chance the rescue ship would pick up more survivors but it would be hours before they would meet the ship.

Several other adults and children were also placed on the wagon and covered with blankets. The men scanned the water and the beaches one more time for survivors or bodies. Afterwards the group started their slow return trip.

The captain's knee was greatly swollen and he continued to wince as the cart hit the bumps in the road. His mind was already preoccupied, however, with the upcoming inquiry into the ship fire. Could he have prevented the disaster? Why was the ship so far away from the shore and why did they lose power so quickly?

Captain Sweet looked at Mr. Watts, his first mate, who walked beside the cart. "We have failed, Mr. Watts, in our responsibilities. I don't know if the fire could have been prevented. I do know the majority of lives would have been saved if the ship had been beached. How did we end up being so far away from land?"

Mr. Watts reminded the captain that the shoreline between Manitowoc and Sheboygan was curved and that the fire had caught them at the furthest point away from the shore. In addition, there were some rocky shoals on the north side of Sheboygan so the first mate set the course to steer far away from them. The first mate concluded, "Our biggest problem was that the *Phoenix* lost power soon after the fire alarm had been sounded. If we had more steam, the ship would have had a chance to reach the shore."

The captain agreed that it was highly unusual to have lost all power so quickly.

"I have already talked to Mr. House for his explanation as to why we lost power so quickly. The engineer was asleep when the fire alarm was sounded. When he got up, the fire was out of control and, shortly after that, the engine went dead. Mr. House thought that perhaps Mr. Owen, the second engineer, had put out the boiler fire to prevent a boiler explosion. The conditions were too hectic, however, for any rational explanation."

Earlier, while waiting on the beach, the captain had questioned the second fireman O'Brien. The fireman described how he first had become aware of the fire but could not explain why the ship lost power. The engines were still running when he was sent topside to raise the alarm. O'Brien next saw the second engineer and the first fireman after their escape from the boiler-room. By that time, Mr. Owen was unconscious while the badly burned and dazed Nugent kept on repeating the same thing, " Mr. Owen, we have to get out of here or we'll die."

The horrific confusing scenes still whirling in his mind, Captain Sweet once again admonished himself and the first mate for failing to carry out their responsibilities.

"We have failed, Mr. Watts, in our responsibilities to save our passengers. Only four cabin passengers reached the beach. I should have never allowed you and Mr. Blish to place me in the lifeboat. After my departure, the ship must have been swept by panic."

The first mate concurred that mayhem started right after the captain had boarded the lifeboat. Still, the two boats had carried forty-three people to shore and could not possibly take any more.

The captain corrected the first mate. "Our primary responsibility was to save the cabin passengers. I do feel sorry for the steerage passengers. However, they paid a lot less money for the passage and were really interchangeable with cargo. No lifeboats were provided for the steerage passengers and there were no legal or moral responsibilities. All captains are honor-bound, however, to save all the cabin passengers before leaving the ship".

After a couple of hours, the Dutch immigrants reached the marshes at the outlet of the Pigeon River. Warily, they took a detour until the river narrowed and they were able to ford it. Soon local children and men appeared, encouraging the stragglers. Finally, the immigrants reached the first homes where people offered them hot drinks.

The horse wagon carrying Captain Sweet made its first stop at Doctor J.J. Brown's home. The captain was carried inside and would stay there until the spring shipping season. Mr. Watts, together with the other crewmen and passengers, continued toward the pier to await the rescue ship. Along the way, food, drinks, and blankets were offered to the survivors. As soon as they had satisfied their needs, they all trudged to the pier.

Meanwhile, The *Delaware*, towing the hulk of the *Phoenix*, was slowly approaching the pier. The immigrants and the crewmen wondered if she was bringing more survivors and if there were any kin or friends among those rescued?

Finally, the rescue ship passed the end of the pier, the scorched hulk straining at the end of the stretched out towline. By then, the top of the *Phoenix* was practically awash. Just a few feet from the partly completed pier, the hulk's bottom hit a sand bar and the ship would exact one more victim. The bursting towing line snapped across the pier striking a boy in the head. His face would be disfigured for the rest of his life.

Mr. Watts was overwhelmed when he recognized the engineer and the clerk plus one passenger from the *Phoenix* standing on the deck of the rescue ship. The three survivors on deck meant that others could still be recovering in the lounge. He shouted, anxious to learn the fate of the remaining crewmen and passengers.

"How many survivors are aboard this ship?"

Mr. House replied, "Only the three of us were picked up by the *Delaware*. Did all three lifeboats reach the shore?"

The reply was not what anybody wanted to hear: only two lifeboats.

The engineer cleared his throat before describing the plight of those who had abandoned the ship, "I saw the third lifeboat swamped with water. I also saw Mr. Blish building a raft for the Dutch children. I was hoping that he would get near the third lifeboat and organize a bailing-out operation. I am sure the Hollanders would do whatever he told them. Perhaps they will still reach the land today or tomorrow...."

The seven surviving crewmen headed back to Dr. Brown's home to make the final reports to the captain. The *Phoenix* was a burned-out hulk aground right next to the pier. The only known survivors were the three aboard the *Delaware* and the forty-three who had reached the land in lifeboats.

Captain Sweet's bad knee was finally properly attended to and the large abscess was drained. While the physical pain was subsiding, it was replaced by the anguish over the missing crewmen and passengers. There was still an urgent need to ascertain all the facts pertinent to the disaster. The *Delaware* would be heading north later that day and the crewmen wanted to leave aboard her. It was the end of the shipping season and it probably was their last chance to get home for winter.

The captain questioned the clerk and the engineer about the developments aboard the ship after the lifeboats had departed.

There was plenty to tell and Mr. Blish's name was mentioned repeatedly. Then there were stories about their own survival in the water. All around them were dozens of passengers and crewmen who one by one succumbed to hypothermia and slid below the waves.

Finally, the captain dismissed the crew except for Mr. Watts, Mr. House, and the fireman O'Brien. One more attempt would be made to find out what caused the fire and why the *Phoenix* had lost the power so quickly.

O'Brien repeated his story of how O'Connor had warned them about the boiler being low on water. The second engineer refused to wake up Mr. House and tried to fix the situation himself. He turned on the second water pump but that did not make any difference.

Mr. House shook his head, stating that valves on the second pump were often set to deliver water to the top deck. When he came out from his cabin, he did notice water on the deck. The only mystery was why the first pump did not deliver enough water. One explanation could have been a fouled inlet.

It remained unclear why the ship had lost power so quickly and was unable to get closer to the shore. Fireman O'Brien had no explanation as he was on the top deck at the time. Mr. House reported that just before the engine stopped, it was running rapidly, as if in a run-away condition. The superheated steam from a boiler low on water was a warning sign of an impending boiler explosion. Perhaps the second engineer had flooded the boiler fire trying to save the ship.

The captain continued his questioning about the cause of the fire and the steps that could have been taken to prevent or contain the damage. Before dismissing the men, he rationalized the cause of the tragedy. "Fires have been and will always remain a grave danger to all ships, especially the steamships. If the second engineer and the first fireman were at fault, they had already paid for it with their lives."

The survivors were fed and given quarters by the people of Sheboygan. The Dutch immigrants remained dazed, incomprehensive of what had happened and still hoping and praying that their relatives and neighbors would show up later that day.

The sailors were offered free drinks at the Merchant Hotel but they spent more time reminiscing than drinking. Their thoughts were with their missing crewmen and they knew it was unlikely that they would be seen again. Sailors took turns telling stories about the absent mates, the heroic Mr. Blish, and finally the tragedy of the Hazelton sisters from Sheboygan.

The hotel manager, who was providing the free drinks, grew pale hearing their account of the two sisters. Without a word, he and his wife turned around and walked away shakily. The sailors were surprised by the man's reaction and asked who the man was. The bartender also appeared shocked and it was a while before he could answer.

"That was Mr. Hazelton, the proprietor of this hotel. His two daughters left in August to go to a boarding school in Buffalo. They did write a letter that they were homesick and would like to come home for the holidays. Still, we did not think they would return until May...."

The *Delaware's* captain was anxious to leave before the end of the day. Except for the captain, all the surviving *Phoenix's* crewmen boarded that ship, eager to get back home for Christmas. An hour after departing Sheboygan, the seven crewmen were on deck scanning the water for any remains from the *Phoenix*. Soon flotsam appeared, as well as thirty to forty bodies. The crewmen pleaded with Captain Tuttle to stop and pick up the corpses so they could have a proper burial.

The captain refused. "The fishing boats will be here soon.

They will have more time to search the area and bring all the bodies to Sheboygan."

The schooner *Liberty* was to travel in the opposite southerly direction but the Milwaukee-bound survivors were not ready to board it yet. There was still hope there would be more survivors. The third lifeboat or a raft could have drifted away and reached shore far away from Sheboygan. It would be unfair to carry the bad news to Mrs. Blish without knowing for sure the fate of her husband. Naturally, the Dutch immigrants were even more reluctant to leave Sheboygan until all hopes were exhausted or the washed up bodies given a burial.

A temporary morgue was set up in an empty store building. During the next few days, only a few bodies were washed ashore and transported to this mortuary. That building became the most often visited place in the village. About two hundred fifty people had been lost but only a couple dozen bodies were recovered. Hollanders were said to carry gold coins sewn into their belts or clothes. Many of them would sink to the bottom, with the lake retaining their corpses forever.

Most Dutch families looked in vain for their missing relatives. Anguish followed when the survivors did find their dead loved ones. One macabre exception was an anguished man who kept inspecting the bodies until he recognized his wife. He then removed her gold cross on a chain plus other valuables and left the area, leaving the task of burying her to others.

The pioneers from the Dutch settlement in the southern part of Sheboygan County started to arrive late in the afternoon to offer help to their countrymen. The survivors told them that they had lost all their money and valuables. The 24 surviving Hollanders spent the winter in Sheboygan County and most of them would continue to live in the area.

Finally, four days after the disaster, the schooner *Liberty* left for Milwaukee, from where the news of the disaster was telegraphed to Chicago and other cities. The O'Connors and Mr. Heath were the only survivors traveling on that ship.

The Geerlings were still in too much shock to travel. Furthermore, their family was spread out between different households providing quarters to the survivors. The family who was hosting one of their daughters insisted on trying to adopt her. It would be months before the Geerlings family would be reunited and able to move on to Milwaukee. It would also take months before the horrible news about the *Phoenix's* tragedy would reach the relatives and neighbors in Holland.

Chapter 20

From Flames and Ashes

Sheboygan in 1885, Sheboygan County Research Center

For days, streams of Sheboygan residents converged on the waterfront to look at the burnt wreck. The *Phoenix'* hulk lay aground in eight feet of water, right next to the pier. The residents knew that most Dutch immigrants had planned to buy land and carried hundreds of dollars in gold coins. Some locals were determined to retrieve the money for their own benefit.

The coroner, James Berry, was the first one to go aboard the ship shortly after the *Phoenix* had come to a rest on the sandbank. There were a number of smoldering bodies on the deck but Berry was more interested in the few gold coins visible in the ashes. The real treasures, however, turned out to be submerged on or beside the keel. Standing in freezing water up to his neck, Berry dived, repeatedly searching for the gold-filled belts. Reports stated that he recovered two belts. Shortly after that, he bought two pedigree cows from the East Coast, starting the county's dairy and cheese traditions. Berry often talked about the *Phoenix* wreck and claimed that many others recovered more than he did.

Cash was scarce in the New Territories but, in Sheboygan, many Dutch and French gold coins, some marked by fire, circulated for months after the disaster. The Hollanders, many of whom jumped into the lifeboats without their coats, seemingly were all left destitute. Rumors floated that some of the passengers were forced to give up their gold-filled belts by the sailors. The fact that the surviving crewmen left the same day on the propeller *Delaware,* only added to the suspicions.

The biggest speculation was about the wealth of the Geerlings family. Some claimed that the Geerlings had carried as much as fifty thousand dollars. The money was supposedly hidden in sea chests and sewn in belts, coats, and the women's dresses. It was even said that the missing daughter and son perished because they had gone back to the steerage compartment to recover the gold-filled coats.

The grief-stricken Geerlings family spent several months in Sheboygan trying to reunite the family. One of their daughters was given shelter by a local family who then demanded the right to adopt her. Eventually the surviving Geerlings reunited and reached Milwaukee where they lived for decades. Gerrit Geerlings never recovered from the shock of the disaster and did not resume his calling as a deacon. The Milwaukee censuses listed his job as a shoemaker and showed the family living in a two thousand dollar home. Some of his children would eventually move to the Dutch settlements in Michigan and Iowa. No Geerlings are currently known to live in Wisconsin.

The rumors about the Geerlings' wealth were probably a

myth. The inherited father-in-law's properties were heavily mortgaged and the last public record in Holland described Geerlings as "not-well-to-do." Geerlings' name did not appear on any transatlantic passenger lists or the American immigration records. Since they were still in Holland during the summer and then traveled with their Enter's neighbors on the *Phoenix*, most likely they all crossed the Atlantic together. Were the passenger records faulty? Or did the family travel under assumed names because of their son who had evaded military service? Or was it because of some unfulfilled financial obligations?

After the disaster, the Landeweerd sisters stayed with the Dutch settlers in the southern part of the Sheboygan County. One of them, Gerdina Schuppert, never recovered from her icy-water ordeal of being towed behind the lifeboat. She died six months later. The young bride Teuntje Wissink nee Landeweerd bore three children in America and then died in 1857 while giving birth to twins. The twenty-year-old pretty Hendrika Landeweerd married Derk Voskuil who used a broom for rowing in his lifeboat. The baby Hanna Landeweerd grew up with Hendrika and eventually married Henry Meengs. At the turn of the 21st century, there would be a total of four hundred descendants of the four sisters.

The Landeweerd sisters were able to bury the body of their mother, who was eventually washed ashore. The corpses of their father, three brothers, and another sister were never recovered. According to the family stories, Hendrika arrived in Sheboygan with a two hundred dollar note, which she used to buy milk for her baby sister. Supposedly, the sellers did not return any change from that note.

Berendina Willink was last seen on the beach but then got separated from her cousin, Derk Voskuil. For over one hundred and fifty years her fate was unknown until her descendant, Harold Schouten and his wife Sylvia, recently traced the old family records. Berendina ended up in Alto, a Dutch settlement forty miles west of Sheboygan where she married Gerrit Veenendaal. They had two daughters but within ten years both Berendina and her husband died.

The lives of the survivors and their relatives were full of intermingled marriages. Teunis Schuppert, whose wife Gerdina nee Landeweerd, died just months after reaching the shore, ended up marrying Geertje Veenendaal, a relative of Berendina's husband. They had several children and then Teunis died unexpectedly. Geertje then married her step brother-in-law, Berend Jan Wissink, also a *Phoenix* survivor. Wissink's first wife was Teuntje nee Landeweerd, a survivor who lived only until 1857.

The three Oonk sisters and their surviving father also settled in the southern part of the Sheboygan County. The bodies of their mother and three brothers were never found. The twenty-two-year-old Johanna married another *Phoenix* survivor Hiram Russelink. They had 2 children before she died 6 years later during childbirth. Her husband would marry two more times to raise a total of 11 children. The seventeen-year-old Harmina later married a Hollander Arend Jan Guerink and her father lived with them. The twelve-year-old Janna, in time, would marry Berend Willem Pietenpol, a local Hollander. The three sisters bore a total of 14 children.

Eventually new lives had to be established. Hendrik Wilterdink lost his invalid wife and 5 children but started a new family in Wisconsin after marrying the family maid, Willemina Ten Dollen.

Only one survivor, Hendrik Jan Esselinkpas, settled in the Dutch community in Michigan. He got married there and had several children. Tired of hearing his name mispronounced, he eventually changed his last name to Pas. Gerritjen Oberink was another survivor who moved away from the Sheboygan County.

She settled in Milwaukee and, in June 1948, married Hendrik Jan Beernink who had come to America in August of 1847. They had 5 children, none of whom lived beyond early childhood. Gerritjen died in 1858.

In Holland, Gerrit and Jozina Te Winkel were devastated when they received the horrible news. Four of their children and Jozina's two sisters had perished in the fire. Jozina felt guilty for not traveling with the children, even though she had become sick just before their departure. She wondered what would have happened if she had allowed her husband to travel with the children and one of her sister? Could he have been able to get them into the lifeboats or would they all perish? Gerrit, together with Jozina, emigrated to America in 1848 and raised a second family of children.

The news about the tragedy was a great shock in Holland. Families mourned their dead relatives. Equally devastated were those who had made vows to join their neighbors and sweethearts the following year. In 1848, Dutch emigration to America dropped by half. Swijtinck, the shipping agent, grieved for all the people he had persuaded to cross the Atlantic. His income fell considerably and two years later, he emigrated with his whole family to America.

Most of the 24 Dutch survivors eventually became prosperous farmers and had large families. For decades they remained silent about their ordeal on that fateful, late November night. In some cases, the survivors started to describe the fire episodes only to their grandchildren. One hundred fifty years later, the Sheboygan County Historical Society issued certificates to four thousand descendants of the *Phoenix* survivors.

Wisconsin would certainly have a lot more residents of Dutch descent if all of the *Phoenix'* passengers had arrived safely. Their success in turn would have encouraged more of their relatives and neighbors to join them here. Sheboygan

County alone could have had thousands of additional residents.

Sheboygan continued to grow and, at the turn of the century, was a major port on the Great Lakes. Often there were more than sixty ships in the harbor. Many of them were bringing in timber and carrying away Sheboygan's famous furniture products.

Most of the Sheboygan's later newcomers were Germans. One immigrant from Austria bought a foundry factory and, in 1883, introduced an enameled "horse trough/hog scalder." A modified version, with four legs added, became hugely popular used as a bathtub. Today, Kohler is internationally known for bathtubs, the American Club five-star resort, and the famous golf courses. The "Whistling Straits" course, host of PGA and Ryder Cup championships, has a spectacular view of Lake Michigan waters where the *Phoenix* burned during the night. Another well-known Sheboygan attraction is the Blue Harbor Resort and Conference center, located just across the river from the final resting place of the burnt *Phoenix* hulk.

While extensive records are available about the *Phoenix's* Dutch immigrants, little is known about the other survivors. The only record of Clarence O'Connor's post-tragedy existence was a letter published in the Milwaukee Journal two months after the disaster. Mr. O'Connor thanked the people of that city for providing his family with shelter and hospitality. An article in Sheboygan mentioned Hamlin Heath's return visit a year after the tragedy.

Captain Sweet spent several months in Dr. Brown's home. The doctor later wrote a lengthy article about the captain's account of the tragedy. Returning to Cleveland, Captain Sweet gave up his maritime career and ran for political offices. T.S. Donahue, the ship's clerk, described his memories of the tragedy in two newspaper articles. One of his statements, where he contends that the steerage passengers were Norwegian, was obviously not accurate.

Mrs. Blish was shocked by the news that her young husband was missing and presumed dead. She asked her brother to travel to Sheboygan to get more information. There were no leads and Blish's body was never recovered.

Mr. and Mrs. Hazelton could not stand the thought that their two daughters died within the sight of their home. Hazelton sold his interest in the Merchant Hotel and moved to an even more removed New Territory: California, where the gold rush was just starting.

Most of the Dutch immigrants settled in the Dutch communities in the southern part of Sheboygan County. The survivors busied themselves with work and refused to talk about the tragedy in which so many of their relatives and friends had died. Their children were warned never to ask questions about the ship fire. After a flurry of the initial newspaper accounts, the disaster became largely forgotten, especially when the civil war preoccupied the public's attention.

Fifty years would pass before the newspapers would again publish more articles to commemorate the anniversary of the tragedy. A number of survivors were still alive and actually quite eager to describe the events, which had taken place so long ago. New details were revealed. Most descriptions were only the fragments that were still retained in their memory. In a few cases, the facts and myths were mixed up.

Twenty years later, a dedicated historian, William O. van Eyck, spent a number of years researching and documenting the story of the *Phoenix's* passengers. More time passed while America's attention was focused on the greater challenges: the Great Depression and the World War II. Eventually the one-hundredth anniversary of the tragedy arrived and some newspaper articles were published. The public commemorations consisted mainly of church services in the Dutch communities.

The number of descendants of the survivor eventually grew into thousands. Some of the great grandchildren wanted to know more of their ancestors and started to collect family stories and carry out genealogical research. Ione and Ron Heinen, the descendants of several survivors, have spent twenty years developing the *Phoenix* historical exhibits, which won awards from the Wisconsin Historical Society.

To commemorate the 150th anniversary of the tragedy, special celebrations were held in Manitowoc and Sheboygan Counties in 1997. Hundreds of the survivors' descendants plus visitors from many states and European countries gathered on the rocky shoals of Sheboygan's North Point. One hundred fifty years earlier, just before dawn, a lighthouse was shining at that site. The lighthouse's beam signaled to the propeller *Phoenix* that they were less than two hours from their destination.

Chapter 21

The Treasure Quest

Sea Chest With Gold Coins, by Thea Textor

The *Phoenix's* hulk was very valuable and readily accessible, submerged in only eight feet of water. The machinery alone was estimated to have a salvage value over two thousand dollars. That was a lot of money in 1847 when cash was scarce and a whole ship like the *Phoenix* could be acquired for less than one thousand dollars. More salvage proceedings would be obtained from the recovered hardware and other cargo, insured for twelve thousand dollars.

In addition, there were the speculations about the gold hidden by the Dutch passengers. Part of it probably remained in the steerage compartment in the sea chests and other hiding places. Most of the gold was sewn into the Hollanders' belts and coats.

Many of those gold-filled coats were left behind in the steerage compartment during the nighttime panic.

Finally, there was the ship's safe box, last seen tumbling into the water a mile or two from the pier. Rumors claimed as much as one hundred thousand dollars of gold were stored in the safe. On the other hand, the ship's clerk made statements that the safe contained only fifteen hundred dollars.

The easy treasure pickings were only on the first day when James Berry and others recovered some gold-filled belts submerged in the water. People came back for days equipped with hoes and shovels to sift the ashes and scrape the submerged bottom of the ship. Piles of worthless debris were recovered as well as some pieces of partially melted gold coins and valuables. In December, an investigator from the insurance company arrived but, by that time, the *Phoenix*'s hulk was covered with many feet of ice.

Legal proceedings over the salvage rights to the *Phoenix* started before the end of December. In court, Captain Tuttle claimed the salvage rights to the hulk and all the cargo. His stated justification was that the ship was abandoned and that he was entitled to such a reward due to the risk and hazard involved in towing the *Phoenix* to shore.

The next spring the machinery and the hardware cargo were recovered and sold. The boiler was not deemed worth the recovery and it ended up rusting on the beach for years. The remaining salvage rights to the hulk were sold for forty dollars to an Englishman by the name of Sutton who pursued a business of hauling goods in the area. The man put up a high fence around the area with a sign "positively no admittance." Sutton's wealth visibly turned for the better and he also ended up adopting a surviving orphan girl from the tragedy. Sometime later, he moved to Chicago where he entered politics and for years was a judge. The little girl was said to have looked after the man and his wife for years afterwards.

Everything connected to the *Phoenix* had a value. During that first winter, some boys skating on the frozen lake saw a metal pipe sticking out. They chipped the ice to recover the ship's part and were later rewarded with twenty-five dollars by sailors who bought this as a souvenir from the disaster.

Eventually the storms broke up the hulk and most sections were washed onto the beach. The scavengers hauled away the timber for firewood and salvaged all iron and brass parts. In those days, even simple nails were hand-made and quite valuable. Pioneers who had to move to a new location often burned their cabins just so they could recover the nails.

The continued interest in the tragedy was a magnet for fraud. The following summer a ship arrived in Sheboygan with a ghoulish load of charred wooden shoes. They were said to have been worn by the *Phoenix's* Dutch passengers and found washed ashore. The Dutch residents quickly declared the shoes to be fake.

Years passed but the memories remained of the gold at the bottom of the lake. Forty-two years after the tragedy, a syndicate of Detroit partners attempted to find the ship's safe. The area where it was reported to have fallen into the water was between eighty and one hundred feet deep, suitable for diving exploration. Newspapers carried the story of the exploration plans but there was no indication that the safe had ever been found.

Interest in the *Phoenix's* wreckage revived after World War II. Several amateur divers searched for wrecks in the harbor and in the nearby waters. One wooden wreck was located in the 1950s. Initially, it was declared to be the *Phoenix* but it turned out to be a smaller sailing ship. Dozens of wooden-hulled ships went down in the Sheboygan area but most were small cargo sailing ships.

More recent research revealed that the lake shoreline had moved east by more than a hundred feet. The original "North" pier, where the hulk had been beached, became covered by soil and the waterfront additions. In the late nineteen nineties, a new boat marina was constructed in that area. Boats tying to the new waterfront were reporting hitting an underwater obstruction. The divers went to investigate and found a few ribs from a ship's hull, which more than likely belonged to the *Phoenix*.

Probably more ship's remains are buried under the new marina's waterfront. Finding the ship's original propeller would have been the best positive identification. The early Erickson propellers had a unique construction and were built only for several years.

One can only wonder what is inside the *Phoenix's* safe and whether it will ever be recovered. The Great Lakes salvage rights are different from those on the open oceans. Currently, it is illegal for divers in Wisconsin to remove any underwater artifacts without a specific permit. Let's hope that the safe will be located and it's contents will be shown to the public in the Sheboygan Museum.

Very few of the victims' bodies were ever recovered. It is thought that many of them had gold coins sewn into their belts and coats and, thus, sank to the bottom of the lake. The location where the passengers jumped into the water could be fairly readily located. The twenty-foot long cast iron ship funnel was reported to have fallen into the water in that area. It could be then readily detected with the underwater magnetic search instruments. The location is about eight miles from Sheboygan and four and a half miles from the shore, with a water depth of roughly one hundred twenty feet.

Perhaps the greatest treasure recovered from the *Phoenix* is the Dutch bible originally carried by the Landeweerd family.

The parents and four of the siblings died in the fire. The four surviving daughters carried the water-stained bible with them. It measures 10 x 16 inches and is 5 inches thick. In 1963, the descendants of the Landeweerd survivors donated the family bible to the Sheboygan County Historical Museum.

Chapter 22

Acknowledgements

Sanderlings Along Lake Michigan, by Thea Textor

The seed for this historical book was first planted several years ago during a family Christmas meal. My son, Alexander, was always interested in diving and was researching the shipwrecks near Sheboygan. He confronted me, however, with a discrepancy.

"Dad, you remember that story you used to tell us about people of Sheboygan watching from the beaches while hundreds of passengers were dying aboard a burning ship?"

I nodded my head, recalling that most of them were immigrants from Holland. My wife and I are not of Dutch descent but we have always found that story fascinating. We live right on Lake Michigan and, on autumn nights, often speculate about the distant lights of the ships passing by. What are their destinations and who is waiting for them?

"Well, the people of Sheboygan could not have watched that ship because it sank eighteen miles south of Sheboygan."

I shook my head stating that his information was probably about a different ship.

"It couldn't have been a different ship. You told us that it happened in the middle of nineteen century, that it was a steamship, and that a lot of Dutch immigrants died in that fire. Those were precisely the facts I found on the ship that had sunk eighteen miles south of Sheboygan. I checked all other shipwrecks in the Sheboygan area and none matched the same facts."

I still felt that the reference to people watching the distant fire was likely to have been factual. Thus, I repeated that there were probably two different tragedies with similar details. The following week, both my son and I spent time searching the Internet. There were, in fact, two similar ship disasters. The burning ship he was referring to was the side-wheeler steamship *Niagara*, which sank in 1856. Approximately one hundred passengers, most of them Dutch, lost lives during that tragedy. There was a good reason why my son initially did not find the *Phoenix* in his diving book. The *Phoenix's* hulk had been towed to shore and most of it was salvaged. Thus, it was not included in the list of Sheboygan-area shipwrecks accessible to divers.

Soon my son was sending me a series of the Internet articles about the *Phoenix* passengers and other immigrants who had come to America during that area. I became engrossed in the lives and the accomplishments of those early pioneers. The *Phoenix* accounts surpassed the story of the Titanic in their rich drama of colorful and heroic characters. Those early heroes deserved a historical book that would tie together the available records and recreate the passengers' hopes and experiences.

My first research contact was with the Dutch historian Jan H. Wissink. He encouraged me to proceed with the project and we exchanged many e-mails since that first contact. Mr. Wissink is the author of a number of many Internet articles, including

"When they came…" and is related to the Wissink survivor from the *Phoenix*. My friend Barbara Silva edited the first few chapters and also encouraged me to proceed with the project. I received more encouragement from Rhea Hartjes who also helped with me with Dutch translations.

As soon as I became convinced that this book was viable, I started to contact the descendants of the survivors. The first to respond were Ronald and Ione Heinen, both of them descendants of several survivors. Twenty years ago, Ione had contacted relatives who were not even aware that they also were the survivors' descendants. Soon she started to accumulate family records and newspaper articles. Her museum exhibits won awards from the Wisconsin Historical Society.

Both Mr. and Mrs. Heinen shared many family stories with me and gave me full access to their extensive and well organized *Phoenix* records. Furthermore, they have edited the first draft of the full manuscript. Ione Heinen has suffered health problems but her cheerful and enthusiastic disposition is a living proof that the *Phoenix* spirit will keep on re-emerging from the ashes.

In 1997 a series of special events were held to commemorate the 150th anniversary of the *Phoenix* odyssey. Hundreds of guests came from many states in America, Holland, and other countries. Dutch television produced a program about the *Phoenix* and Sheboygan County. Earlier, the Dutch queen attended banquets in Cedar Grove and other communities where many old Dutch pioneers had settled. A short but comprehensive booklet "Out of the *Phoenix*… A Tragic Beginning" was reprinted several times and is still available at the Sheboygan County Research Center and the Sheboygan County Historical Museum.

The 1997, celebration helped to resurrect the memory of the tragedy and the survivors' dreams fulfilled through their descendants. The Sesquicentennial Committee, most of whom were the descendants of the survivors, did an outstanding job. The committee included Mary K. Risseeuw, Ron and Ione Heinen, Dale and Judith (Mentink) Brasser, Norman and Marjorie (Ten Haken) Mulder, Mildred J. Wieberdink, Mary Lou (Harmelink) Du Mez, Darlene J. (Harmelink) Navis, Lorraine (Bennin) Boldt, Marvin and Rose (Wissink) Duenk, Joseph and Gladys (Oosterhuis) Wisse, Stanley and Sue (Repenshek) Wilterdink, and Mark and Janice (De Blaey) Hesselink.

The *Phoenix* fire will be always remembered as the greatest tragedy suffered by any immigrant group arriving in America. Compared to other 19th century ship disasters, there is a lot more information available about the *Phoenix's* passengers and the ship's final moments. Right after the tragedy, the newspapers in Sheboygan, Milwaukee, and other cities printed a number of lengthy articles. One of them described the story as told by Captain Sweet to Dr. J.J. Brown in whose home the captain had remained for several days. There were also first hand accounts by the ship's clerk and other witnesses. A few letters by the survivors and witnesses also survived.

For years the Dutch survivors did not talk about the tragedy and the children were warned not to ask questions which could bring up the bad memories. As the fiftieth anniversary approached, the newspapers published a number of articles interviewing the survivors and quoting new details.

In the 1920s, William O. Van Eyck devoted years of his life to the *Phoenix* research and interviews with the children of the survivors. In 1923, he published a lengthy article, "The Story of the Propeller *Phoenix*" and donated his research material to the Dutch museum in Holland, Michigan.

More recently Mary Risseeuw has done extensive research in this country and in Holland to add names and family information. Some of the passengers previously omitted, or listed as wife or child, became known by name. Her articles are available on Internet, including "The Lost Are Found – A New Perspective on the Passengers of the *Phoenix*."

Yvette Hoitink, a researcher from Holland, has researched the *Phoenix* passengers' lives in Holland and created excellent Internet websites. She has visited Sheboygan in the past and remains helpful to those in quest of more information.

The Sheboygan County Historical Research Center in Sheboygan Falls has an extensive collection of information on the *Phoenix*. It includes old newspaper articles, letters, and the histories of the survivors' families. The SCHR also has a great staff who has been very helpful on this project.

The Sheboygan historian, Bill Wangemann, has written numerous newspaper, Internet articles, and books. His "The Loss of the *Phoenix*" article is a very stirring account of that journey. He also provided me with some background information and encouraged me to continue with this project.

Mrs. William Koelpin kindly granted me the right to reproduce her late husband's dramatic painting of the burning *Phoenix*. William Koelpin has been well known for wildlife paintings which are available from the website gallery www.americansportingarts.com. The *Phoenix* painting combines his artistic talents and the knowledge of fire drama from his past experience as a firefighter.

Finally, I want to thank my wife Carol, my son Alexander, and my two daughters for their support and help in preparing this book. Thea, a recent graduate from Harvard, completed a thorough edit of my manuscript with many suggestions on better transitions and improved narrations. Julia, a new teacher from U of W-Madison, had helpful suggestions concerning the character development. Alexander, who originally inspired me to write this book, has done a great job doing most of the research on the *Phoenix*. He also prepared the map plus assisted and inspired me in many other areas. Mrs. Rosalind M. Hack, an ex-English teacher/editor and a cheerful teammate in bridge tournaments, did the final editing.

Each year more and more families are honoring the memory the *Phoenix* passengers. The descendants of the Landeweerd family have held an annual commemorative picnic for years. The Sikkink family all perished in the fire but their relatives settled in Wisconsin and also kept the tradition of annual gatherings. Spurred by the annual newspaper articles published on the anniversary of the tragedy, more people are tracing their roots and contacting the descendants of the survivors.

Recently, Ms. Nancy Potter from Waunakee, Wisconsin visited Sheboygan to show off an old quilt. A section of the quilt included the following writing, "Dedicated to the memory of our cousin Edwin West who perished in a ship fire in 1847." Until that point, the first name of Mr. West did not appear in any records. Hopefully, with the publication of this book, the readers will provide additional new information about the passengers and the crew.

A few final comments on the methodology used by the author. All names used in this book are from the historical records. The only exception is the first name of the younger Hazelton sister. Most records simply refer to them as the Hazelton sisters and only one old letter states the name of one of the sisters as Eliza. Both sisters had an important role in this tragedy and thus a popular name from that period, Anne, has been picked for the other sister.

Hendrikus Swijtinck was a real shipping agent who was very active in the Winterswijk province. There are no records showing that he had sold tickets to all the Seceder groups traveling aboard the frigate *France* and the propeller *Phoenix*. It was convenient, however, to use Swijtinck to introduce the various groups and explain the life in the New Territories in America.

The shipping agents did have an important role in motivating the Dutch people to emigrate to America. The Dutch historian Jan Wissink provided the shipping agent's name and information that, in 1850, Swijtinck emigrated with his family to America.

The details about the shipboard conditions during the transatlantic crossing came from a number of old letters describing the voyages during that era. Additional information was provided by Andrew Gantt who had crossed the Atlantic several times in a sailboat. The descriptions of the travel on the Hudson River and the Erie Canal came from a number of old and contemporary voyage descriptions.

Information about the *Phoenix's* docking location in Manitowoc the evening before the disaster, came from Dale Brasser. A descendant of the *Phoenix's* survivors, he provided me with an 1850 Manitowoc port map. Dale and his wife, Judith, also took me on a tour to point out the location of the old pier and the changes in the shoreline and the river channel.

This fascinating story about the fateful journey of the *Phoenix's* passengers is a tribute to the courageous ancestors. They risked their lives crossing the Atlantic, driven by dreams that their families would enjoy freedom and prosperity in the new world.

Chapter 23

Eight Life Stories and Photos
of Some of the Survivors

Prepared by Ione Heinen,
a descendant of two survivors

The first wooden church after emigration,
Wissink's "Why They Came...."
http://web.inter.nl.net/hcc/wissink/why.htm

HARMINA OONK GEURINK
born 1832 – died 1853

Harmina Oonk was a passenger aboard the *Phoenix* traveling with her parents, three brothers, and two sisters. Her brothers and mother all died in the fiery accident.

Her father, Jan Willem Oonk, survived with her two sisters, Johanna Ooonk Ruselink and Janna Hendrika Oonk Pietenpol. Jan Willem Oonk made his home with Harmina and her husband, Arend Jan Geurink. Harmina and Arend Jan Geurink were the parents of three children: Jane Guerink (spouse William Daane), Eliza Guerink (spouse Peter Jensema), and Henry Guerink (spouse Aafke/Effie Jensema).

Although Harmina and her husband Arend Jan, as well as her father, Jan Willem Oonk, settled west of Gibbsville, her descendants have spread out over much of Wisconsin and the United States. Many, however, remain in Sheboygan County as well.

JANNA HENDRIKA OONK PIETENPOL

born 1835 – died 1903

Janna Hendrika Oonk was a teenager when she survived the devastating *Phoenix* accident. She was traveling with her family: parents, three brothers, and two sisters. Her father, Jan Willem Oonk, and two sisters survived. Her mother and brothers were victims to this cruel Lake Michigan disaster.

Family stories tell us the sight of fire terrified Janna Hendrika her entire life. This indelible memory stayed with her forever. She settled west of Gibbsville in the town of Lima with her father and sisters.

When a young lady, she married Berend Willem Pietenpol and remained in the town of Lima, west of Gibbsville, settling on a farm in the area.

Janna Hendrika and Berend Willem, most often called William Pietenpol, were the parents of nine children. One of these children died in childhood.

Their adult children were Jane Pietenpol (spouse William Heule), Johanna Pietenpol (spouse Adrian/Ed Brasser), Henry Pietenpol (spouse Robelia/Ruby Allen), Josephine Wilhelmina Pietenpol (spouse Jacob Brasser), John Pietenpol (spouse Nellie Davis), Benjamin William Pietenpol (spouse A. Lena Kruizenga), Katherina Pietenpol (spouse William Rauwerdink), and William Pietenpol (spouse Hattie Wilterdink).

Large number of descendants of this survivor live in Sheboygan County and throughout the United States.

HANNA GERDINA LANDEWEERD MEENGS

born 1844 – died 1915

Hanna Gerdina Landeweerd was a two and half year old child at the time of the *Phoenix* disaster. She was in the company of her parents, four sisters, and four brothers. Two of her sisters were already married and were aboard with their spouses.

Her parents, brothers, and one sister were victims of the fire. Hanna was thrown into the arms of one of her older sisters and was raised by one of these sisters, Hendrika Landeweerd. At the age of 12, she began supporting herself by working as hired girl for various families.

Ultimately she married Henry Meengs and became the mother of eight daughters. Two of these daughters, Rose and Alice, did not reach mature adulthood.

Her remaining daughters were Delia Meengs (spouse William van der Laan), Elizabeth Meengs, Mary Meengs (spouse Garret John Hilbelink), Henriette Meengs (spouse Matthew J. De Master), Anna Meengs (spouse Benjamin Wissink), and Jennie Meengs (spouse William John Hilbelink).

A great many of her descendants have remained in Sheboygan County in the town of Holland. Cedar Grove, town of Lima, Gibbsville, Hingham, Oostburg, Sheboygan Falls, and Sheboygan. One of her daughters, Delia Meengs van der Laan, moved to the Baldwin area and many of these family members are in that area.

Hanna is shown with her husband, Henry Meengs.

DERK ANTHONIE and

born 1817 – died 1901

HENDRIKA LANDEWEERD VOSKUIL

born 1828 – died 1884

Derk Anthonie Voskuil and Hendrika Landeweerd boarded the *Phoenix* as a single young people in the company of family members.

Derk's family included his sister and her husband, and five children. Hendrika Landeweerd was accompanying the Landerweerd clan. Derk's sister and her entire family were lost as were some of Landeweerd's family members.

Perhaps Derk and Hendrika became acquainted while making their long journey to Sheboygan County or perhaps the common tragedy of surviving the shipwreck brought them together. Whatever the reason, they were the first couple to be married in Cedar Grove in 1848. Hendrika had the added responsibility of raising her younger sister Hanna who also survived.

Derk Anthonie and Hendrika Landeweerd Voskuil had a large family of eleven children. They were Jan Willem Voskuil (spouse (1) Aletta Sweemer, (2) Nancy Serier), Hendrik/Henry Voskuil (spouse Nancy Willemina Meerdink), Berent Willem/William Berend Voskuil (spouse Jane Gertrude Veldboom), Gerdina/DeliaVoskuil (spouse Derk Jan Meengs, Tonia/Cena Voskuil, Gesina/Julia Voskuil (spouse Hendrik John Renskers), Gerrit Voskuil (spouse Henrietta Johanna Blekkink), Derk Hendrik Voskuil (spouse Delia Christina Blekkink), Hannah Voskuil (spouse Abraham Blekkink), Elizabeth Voskuil (spouse Peter Verhulst), and Jahannes/Joe Voskuil (spouse Madge Smith).

Descendants of Derk Anthonie and Hendrika Voskuil are living throughout the United States, with many of them still living in Sheboygan County.

BEREND JAN WISSINK
born 1813 – died 1886

Berend Jan Wissink was sometimes known as Jan Berend Wissink.

He was traveling with his young wife, Teuntje Landeweerd, and Teuntje's family to Wisconsin to establish a home in Sheboygan County with his bride.

Fatefully, they, too, boarded the *Phoenix* at Buffalo, N.Y. to complete the last leg of their journey. As stated elsewhere, the Landeweerd family suffered loss of family members to this unfortunate holocaust, causing the death of Teuntje's parents, four brothers, and a sister.

Berend Jan and Teuntje Wissink built a cabin in the town of Holland. Teuntje died in 1857 after giving birth to twin daughters who also died in infancy. Besides the twins, Berend Jan and Teuntje were the parents of three other children: Jane Henrietta Wissink (spouse Benjamin [Jan Berend] Wynveen), John Wissink, and Gerret Wissink (spouse Jane Fredericka Sikkink).

After Teuntje's death, Berend Jan remarried his sister-in-law, Geritje Veenendaal Schuppert. Geritje was the second wife and widow of Teunis Schuppert, also a *Phoenix* survivor. Teunis Schuppert's first wife was Hendrina, also known as Gerdina Landeweerd, another *Phoenix* survivor (who died months later, never recovering from the ordeal in the frozen water) and a part of the before mentioned Landeweerd clan.

Berend Jan and Geritje Wissink were the parents of five more children. One daughter died as a toddler, while the remaining children were: Tena Wissink (spouse Evert Jan Hyink), Teunis Wissink (spouse Jane Renskers), Mary Wissink, and Barney Henry Wissink (spouse Marie Hilk Scholten).

Many of these descendants have remained in Sheboygan County. Some have moved to the Baldwin area in Wisconsin and throughout the United States

HIRAM JAN RUSELINK
born 1815 – died 1896

Early records give Hiram's name as Harmen Jan Rueselink. Hiram was part of a family entourage when the family departed from the Netherlands in 1847. Apparently Hiram was the only family member to board the *Phoenix*.

Hiram related some time after the accident that he recalled three small lifeboats being discharged from the burning inferno. The third lifeboat supposedly capsized when it was overloaded, drowning all of its passengers. However, information cannot substantiate or disprove this.

Hiram's first wife was also a *Phoenix's* survivor, namely Johanna Oonk. Johanna died in 1853 leaving Hiram with two small daughters to raise, Jane Ruselink (spouse Herman J. Ter Haar), and Gazena Cena Ruselink (spouse Herman Garret Snoeyenbos). After Johanna's death, Hiram married Elizabeth Jansen. She bore him four more children, Henry Ruselink (spouse (1) Flora Follett (2) Mabel Hibbard), William Ruselink (spouse Dolly Case), Catherine Ruselink (spouse Henry Ruselink), and Albert Ruselink (spouse Martha Bos).

Unfortunately, Elizabeth died about ten years after her marriage to Hiram Jan Ruselink leaving him with very small children to raise with the youngest being just an infant. Hiram then married a third time, this time to his cousin Johanna Ruselink. Together they were the parents of seven additional children but two of these children, both sons, died as toddlers.

The children of Hiram Jan and Johanna Ruselink who reached adulthood were: Garret Ruselink (spouse Phoebe Jane Stemerdink), Minnie Ruselink (spouse David Wolfert), John Ruselink (spouse Mary Wilterdink), Elizabeth Ruselink (spouse Jacob Eernisse), and Mary Ruselink (spouse Lewis Faas).

Hiram Jan Ruselink was one of the organizers of the Gibbsville Reformed Church and served as one of the congregation's first elders. Hiram Jan is shown with his third wife, Johanna Ruselink Ruselink.

HENDRIK JAN and

born 1807 – died 1891

WILLEMINA TEN DOLLEN WILTERDINK

born 1829 – died 1914

The Wilterdink family was aboard the *Phoenix* anticipating a new life in Sheboygan County. But tragedy struck the family before they ever reached their destination. Hendrik Jan Wilterdink was traveling in the company of his invalid wife, nee Janna Willemina Mennikk, five children, four sons and one daughter, and the family maid, Willemina Ten Dollen.

Family stories indicate there were only two small lifeboats available for the distressed, panic-stricken passengers aboard the burning ship. Hendrik Jan Wilterdink was rescued in one of the small lifeboats and Willemina Ten Dollen was carried ashore in the other lifeboat.

His wife and the five children perished in the horrible wreck. Besides his family, Wilterdink lost all his financial resources. Unable to speak the language, which was a problem for all the survivors, Wilterdink married Miss Ten Dollen and settled in the town of Lima, west of Gibbsville.

They were some of the first members of the West Gibbsville Baptist Church. Out of their tragic circumstances, they began a new life and were the parents of eight children: Janna/Jane Wilterdink (spouse John Oosterhuis), George Wilterdink (spouse Hannah Bloemers), Hannah Wilterdink (spouse Peter Stokdyk), Gertrude Wilterdink (spouse Jacob Oosterhuis), William Wilterdink (spouse Elizabeth H. Voskuil), Henry J. Wilterdink (spouse Dinah Eernisse), John Wilterdink (spouse Elizabeth Eernisse), and Eliza Wilterdink (spouse William Bennink).

Hundreds of the descendants of these brave survivors, Hendrik Jan and Willemina Ten Dollen Wilterdink still live in Sheboygan County, in the town of Lima, Sheboygan Falls, Gibbsville, Oostburg, Hingham, Cedar Grove, and Sheboygan.

HENDRICK JAN ESSLINKPAS

born 1812 – died 1901

Hendrick Jan Esslinkpas was a single 34 year old young man when he boarded the ill-fated *Phoenix*.

He was traveling in the company of his sister-in-law and her young family. Hendrick Jan's brother, Jan Berend Esslinkpas, died on the first leg of the voyage when these immigrants were sailing the Atlantic aboard the *France* prior to reaching America's eastern shores.

Unfortunately, Hendrick Jan's extended family (sister-in-law and her children) perished. Some family stories tell us Hendrick Jan worked in Sheboygan County the winter of 1847-1848 and continued via land to Holland, Michigan, where he established his roots.

He was the only *Phoenix* survivor to settle in Holland, Michigan. After settling, he married, only to lose his first wife and child in childbirth. He then married a young widow, Gerritje Damkot Kooyers, the mother of two young children. Together they raised Gerritje's children along with their four children, namely: Janna Geertru/Jane Esslinkpas (spouse Henry Kooyers), Johanna/Anne Esslinkpas (spouse William Venhuizen), Samuel Esslinkpas (spouse Mary Schaap), and Jacob Esslinkpas (spouse (1) Reka Boeve and (2) Bertha Hope Nichols).

Tired of his name being misspelled and mispronounced, Esslinkpas shortened his surname to Pas and bequeathed it to his descendants.

Most of Hendrick Jan's descendants live in Michigan and Iowa. He is pictured with his second wife and mother of his children, Gerritje Damkot Kooyers Esslinkpas.

Chapter 24

The Phoenix — Lost and Saved

Crew Lost — total 15
Newell Merrill, second mate, Ohio City
William Owen, second engineer, Toledo
D. W. Keller, steward, Cleveland
J. C. Smith, saloon keeper, Buffalo
Hugh Robinson, first porter, Chicago
John Nugent, first fireman, Buffalo
Thomas Halsey, deckhand
George ———, deckhand
Thomas Fartui, deckhand, River St. Clair
John and August Murdock, deckhands,
    Scotchmen, Canada
Luther Southward, wheelsman, New Bedford
Horace Tisdale, cabin boy
Two colored cooks

Crew Saved — total 8
Captain Benjamin G. Sweet, Cleveland
H. Watts, first mate, Cleveland
M. H. House, engineer, Cleveland
T. S. Donahue, clerk, River St. Clair
G. Kelso, wheelsman, Ohio City
John Mann, deckhand, Cleveland
E. Watts, second porter, Cleveland
Michael O'Brien, fireman, Buffalo

Cabin Passengers Lost — 20

Eliza Hazelton and her sister, Sheboygan, WI
David Blish, Southport (Kenosha, WI)
Mr. Fink and wife, Southport (Kenosha, WI)
Mr. Edwin West, wife, and child, Racine, WI
Mrs. J. Long and child, Milwaukee, WI
Heath, (wife) Sarah Ann plus child
Heath, (father) Joseph Jr., Binghampton, NY
Austin, Amanda (Sarah's sister), "
Austin, Ramsey (Sarah's brother), "
Austin, David and one child
J. Burrows, Chicago, IL
plus probably 2 other unidentified passengers

Cabin Passengers Saved — 5
Clarence O'Connor, wife, & daughter, Ireland

Mr. J. Long, Milwaukee, Milwaukee, WI
Heath, Hamlin S., Binghampton, NY
(on the way to Bureau Co. Illinois)

Steerage Passengers Lost - 219
145 Dutch, 7 Irish, plus as many as 67 Other

Steerage Passengers Saved - 33
24 Dutch+9 Other

Lost From Enter, Holland

children: Willem, age 17
Hendrikje, age 14

Saved From, Enter, Holland
Geerlings, Gerrit, miller, age 44 (died 1886)
Wife: Aaltje (Eliza) de Vries, age 45 (d.1886)
children: Henry (Hendrik John), age 10 (d.1901)
Jacob, age 8 (died 1906)
Altje, age 4 (died 1898)
Gerritje, age 3 (died 1893)

Hommers, Gerrit Jan, age 58, widower farmer
children: Jan, age 33
Gerrit, age 17
Hendrikus, age 12
Lubbers, Hendrikus, age 41, shoemaker
wife: Maria (Marijke), age 46
children: Hendrik (Hein), age 6
Lucas, age 4

Lost From Winterswijk, Holland
Koffers, Teunis, age 52, farmer
wife: Berendina Damkot, age 54
children: Gerrit Jan, age 27
Tobias, age 24
Janna, age 21
Jan Willem, age 15
Johanna, age 12
Wilterdink, (wife) Janna Meenink, age 44
children: Gerrit, age 11
Janna, age 9
Jan Albert, age 7
Berend, age 2
Jan Hendrik, age 1
Wilterdink, Derk, age 41, farmer
wife: Hanna Verink, age 31
children: Anna, age 15
Gerrit, age 2

Saved From Winterswijk, Holland

Wilterdink, Hendrik, (husband) age 40, d.1891
family maid: Willemina Ten Dolle, age 18,
(married Hendrik in Wisconsin -died 1914)

Note: Henrik and Derk were cousins. Hendrik's
brother Jan and his bride crossed the Atlantic on
the same ship but stayed in New York for the
winter. Another cousin and his mother also
remained in New York

Lost From Winterswijk, Holland (contd.) Saved From Winterswijk, Holland (contd.)

Farmhand: Gerrit Bloemers, age 17
Siebelink, Hendrik, age 41, farmer
  wife: Johnanna Ten Broeke, age 44
  children: Janna, age 12
           Gerrit, age 9
  maid: Janna Oonk, age 19
  farmhand: Gerrit Grevers, age 26
Oonk, Gerrit, age 32, farmer
  wife: Harmina Hesselink, age 41
  children: Jan Willem, age 6
           Gerrit, age 3
Oonk, (wife) Janna Damkot, age 51   Oonk, (husband) Jan Willem, age 52
  sons: Jan Willem, age 26   daughters: Johanna, age 22 (died 1853)
           Jan Hendrik, age 20   Harmina, age 15 (died 1904)
           Steven Jan, age 18   Janna, age 12 (died 1903)
Sikkink, Jan Albert, age 36, farmer
  wife: Aleida Weenink, age 41
  children: Tobias, age 12
           Johanna, age 10
           Jan Derk, age 5
           Joanna, age 1
Onnink, Hendrik, age 29, farmer
  wife: Hendrika Ten Haken, age 24
  children: Janna Geertruid, age 4
           Hendrik Jan, age 3
           Berendina Willemina, age 2
  Farmhand: Reessink, Jan Hendrik, age 19
Guerkink, Gerrit, widower, age 42, farmer
  children: Janna Willemina, age 21
           Stijntjen, 19
           Janna Berendina, age 11
           Jan Hendrik, age 9
           Jan Willem, age 6
Kooyers (Koijers), Hendrik, age 46
  wife: Janna Berendina Wilterdink, age 47

children: Engelina, age 12
          Berend, age 11
Nijweide, Hendrik Jan, age 36, farmer
   wife: Dora Voskuil, age 36   Voskuil, (brother) Derk Antony, age 30,
   children: Janna Hendrika, age 10   (died 1901)
          Jan Willem, age 7   Willink, Berendina, age 36, (died 1857)
          Berendina, age 5   (step-daughter of Derk's and Dora's uncle)
          Engelbarts, age 4
          Christina, age 2
Esselinkpas, (wife) Johanna Ten Pas, age 38   Esselinkpas, (brother-in-law) Hendrik Jan,
(husband Jan Berend Esselinkpas died on the ocean voyage)   age 35 (died 1901)
   children: Steven Jan, age 11
          Hendrika, age 9
          Janna Geertruid, age 7
          Willemina, age 5
          Jan Hendrik, age 3
Meenink, (wife) Janna Willemina, age 34
   children: Gerrit Jan, age 11
          Janna Gesiena, age 9
          Jan Albert, age 7
          Berend Willem, age 2
          Jan Hendrik, age 1
Te Winkel, children: Tobias Hendrik, age 7   Note: due to sickness, the parents traveled to
          Gerrit Jan, age 5   America in 1848; the children traveled with the
          Janna Geertruida, age 3   two sisters of the mother (Ten Haken)
          Gerrit Willem, age 1
Ten Haken, Berendina, age 27
Ten Haken, Geertruid, age 19

                              Reuselink, Harman Jan, age 32 (died 1896)

<u>Lost From Aalten, Holland</u>   <u>Saved From Aalten, Holland</u>
Kraayenbrink, Willem, age 37
   wife: Theodora Krienen, age 28
   children: Gerrit Hendrik, age 7
          Johanna, age 3
          Kaatjen, age 2
Navis, Derk Willem, farmer, age 46

Lost From Aalten, Holland (contd.)   Saved From Aalten, Holland (contd.)

wife: Johanna Rexwinkel, age 46
mother: Janna Lieftink, age 79
children: Hendrika Johanna, age 20
             Gerrit Hendrik, age 14
             Hendrik Jan, age 11
             Geertruid, age 8
             Hendrik Willem, age 5
Brusse, Jan, farmer, age 28

Lost From Wisch/Varsseveld, Holland   Saved From Wisch/Varsseveld
Colebrander, Arend, farmer, age 32
wife: Christina Gesink, age 34
children: Grada Aleida, age 13
             Jan Adolf, age 10
             Christina, age 8
             Gerrit Jan, age 6
             Aaltjen, age 4
             baby born 1847
Oberink, Lammert, farmer, age 58
wife: Willemina Hofs, age 55
children: Evert Jan, age 24   Oberink, Gerritje, age 22 (died 1858)
             Grada, age 13
             Hendrik Willem, age 9
             Gerrit Jan, age 19
Te Kotte, Hendrik Jan, farmer, age 56
wife: Aaltjen Nagel, age 55
children: 4 (from Varsseveld immigration records)
Wildenbeest, Roelof
wife: Berendina Radstake
children: Dina Johanna, age 6
Gielink, Derk
wife
1 child
Nebbelink,
wife

| Lost From Wisch/Varsseveld, Holland (contd.) | Saved From Wisch/Varsseveld (contd.) |

Lost From Wisch/Varsseveld, Holland (contd.)   **Saved From Wisch/Varsseveld** (contd.)

2 children:
Toebes.
 wife
 2 children

Lost From Gendringen & Oosterbeek   **Saved From Gendringen & Oosterbeek**
Demkes – Anskink, Catharina
 child: Gerrit Hendrik, age 32
Bruijel, Hendrikus
 wife: Jeneken Bongers
 children: Dirkje
         Hendrina
         Geertruy Willemina
         Derk Willem

Lost From Holten, Overijssel, Holland   **Saved From Holten, Overijssel**
Beumer, Egbert, tailor, age 38
 wife: Harmien Stevens, age 38
 child: Janna, age 3
Beumer, Teunis, tailor, age 50
Landeweerd, Hendrik Eigbert, farmer, age 51
 wife: Gerritdina Hakkink, age 50
 children: Berend Willem, age 17   2 single plus 2 married daughters:
            Tonia, age 14   Landeweerd, Hendrika, age 19 (died 1884)
            Egbert, age 11   Landeweerd, Hanna Gerdina, age 3, d.1915
            Fenneke, age 9

                                 Wissink, Berend Jan, age 34, (died 1886)
                                    wife: Teuntje Landeweerd, age 22 (died 1857)
                                 Schuppert, Teunis, age 23, (died 1856)
                                    wife: Gerdina Landeweerd, age 24 (d. 1848)
                                    child: Dena Johanna, age 2 (died 1916)

Lost - Other Steerage Passengers   **Saved - Other Steerage Passengers**
Irish family of seven   One Irish girl
Plus as many as 67 other unidentified passengers 8 other unidentified steerage passengers

Excellent records exist for the passengers from Holland who traveled in groups and knew each other. Twenty-four Dutch immigrants were saved and at least one hundred forty five were lost. It is possible that a few Hollanders from smaller communities traveled on their own. The survivors from the main Dutch groups did not necessarily account for all of the lost countrymen. The records of the steerage passengers from other countries are almost nonexistent. Only one reference exists of an Irish girl wailing on the beach for her seven lost relatives. There were eight other surviving unidentified steerage passengers.

Three survivors were picked up from the water and forty-three reached the shore in two lifeboats. The *Phoenix* commemorative marker lists the number of survivors as forty-five rather than forty-six. That's because one woman had never recovered from her ordeal in the freezing water and died six months later.

It is interesting that the ship's clerk has referred to the steerage passengers as mostly Norwegians. Quite possibly he had some dealings with a talkative Norwegian passenger (a survivor?) and assumed that the other steerage passengers were also from Norway.

There are many references from the surviving crewmen that there were close to three hundred passengers and crewmen aboard the ship. There were twenty-three crewmen and approximately twenty-five cabin passengers. This would suggest, that in addition to the Hollanders, there were as many as sixty-seven additional steerage passengers lost. Most ships traveling to Wisconsin and Illinois would carry the immigrant families from Germany. Young farm workers or laborers, especially earlier immigrants from Europe, were also likely to travel in the steerage section. The ships' captains often understated the number of the steerage passengers in order not to report the full income to all the ship owners.

Historical Perspective

Many people consider the sinking of the Titanic to be the greatest maritime disaster. Actually, more than a dozen disasters involved considerably higher casualties. Below is a list of some of the great maritime disasters. Each tragedy was unique. The sad part is that most of the casualties could have been prevented.

Great Wartime Maritime Disasters

YEAR	DEAD	SAVED	SHIP & CIRCUMSTANCES
1945	9600	966	Wilhelm Gustloff-German refugees sunk by Soviet S-13 submarine near Gotenhafen/Gdynia
1945	4500	659	General von Steuben-German refugees sunk by the above submarine
1945	7000+	165	Goya-German refugees sunk by Soviet L-3 submarine
1945	7000+	350	Cap Arcona+2other German ships (allied prisoners) sunk by British
1944	5620+	880+	Junyo Maru/Japan (allied POWs)- sunk by British submarine
1944	5600	600	Toyama Maru-Japanese troops sunk by American submarine
1944	4998	1600+	Ryusei Maru/Japan-sunk by American submarine
1944	3000+	500	Tango Maru/Japan (allied POWs)-sunk by American submarine
1940	3000+	2477	RMS Lancastria/England-sunk by German warplanes
1944	2571	267	Rigel-Norway/Germany (allied POWs)- sunk by British warplanes

Great Peacetime Maritime Disasters

YEAR	DEAD	SAVED	SHIP & CIRCUMSTANCES
1981	3000+	21	Dona Paz-overcrowded Philippine ferry collided with a ship
2002	1800	64	Joola-overcrowded Senegalese (Africa) ferry sank in a storm
1865	1700	300+	Sultana-boiler explosion: riverboat full of returning veterans

1912	1500+	706	Titanic-the "unsinkable" English ship collided with an iceberg
1954	1155	159	Toya Maru-Japanase ferry sank during a typhoon
1904	1021+	421	General Slocum-fire struck a church's picnic cruise in New York
1915	1012	473	Empress of Ireland-English ship collided with a freighter in fog
1994	852	137	Estonia-Swedish/Estonian ferry sank in a storm (loose ramp)
1915	845	1650+	Eastland-overloaded Chicago day cruise ship tipped 20ft from shore

FOR REFERENCE

| 1847 | 250+ | 46 | Phoenix-Great Lakes' steamship lost due to fire and human error |

We can assume that the great wartime disasters will never again be repeated. It is not likely that ships will ever again be used to transport large groups of troops, refugees, or prisoners-of-war, as was the case during the two world wars. The peacetime maritime disasters continue, however, to this very day. Large cruise ships and ferries carry a growing number of passengers. Better technology is often offset by continual human error.

Each maritime disaster should have served as a lesson to prevent similar calamities but that has rarely been the case. The *Phoenix* fire, sometimes described as the greatest tragedy befallen on any single immigrant group, was followed by many other similar fire disasters. Even today, some captains still do not slow down in bad weather or refuse to give way when passing another ship. The *Phoenix* tragedy did have one impact on the maritime traditions. The newspaper articles incited a public uproar concerning the *Phoenix's* captain abandoning the ship early. As a result, the tradition of the captain being the last one to leave the ship is enshrined in history.

CONTACT THE AUTHOR

Visit out website: www.phoenix1847.com
and check out our links to other Internet websites with historical and genealogical information about the Phoenix

If you have comments or new information about the *Phoenix's* passengers or crew, please contact the author.
E-mail the author at: **JTextor@phoenix1847.com**
or write to:

Sanderling Press
PO Box 436
Sheboygan, WI 53082-0436

Museums, libraries, schools, and other organizations may contact the author to arrange a presentation about the *Phoenix* and other great maritime disasters.

For additional copies of this book, ask for it at your local bookstore (ISBN# 0-9773710-0-X).
It can also be ordered on Internet: www.phoenix1847.com or by mail:

ORDER FORM

Please send _copies of "Phoenix- The Fateful Journey" at $22.95 each plus $4.00 shipping (Wisconsin residents add $1.15 sales tax per book).
My check or money order for $_____ is enclosed.
Name_____
Address_____
City/State/ZIP_____
Sanderling Press, PO Box 436, Sheboygan, WI 53082-0436